LEGAL ACCOUNTABILITY
IN THE NURSING PROCESS

LEGAL ACCOUNTABILITY IN THE NURSING PROCESS

Irene Murchison, R.N., B.S., M.A.

Thomas S. Nichols, A.B., M.S., LL.B.

Rachel Hanson, R.N., B.S.N.E., M.S.

SECOND EDITION

The C. V. Mosby Company

ST. LOUIS • TORONTO • LONDON   1982

MOSBY

A TRADITION OF PUBLISHING EXCELLENCE

Editor: Pamela Swearingen
Editorial assistant: Bess Arends
Manuscript editor: Patricia J. Milstein
Design: Susan Trail
Production: Kathleen Teal

Second edition

The C.V. Mosby Company
11830 Westline Industrial Drive, St. Louis, Missouri 63141

Library of Congress Cataloging in Publication Data

Murchison, Irene A.
    Legal accountability in the nursing process.

    Bibliography: p.
    Includes index.
        1. Nursing—Law and legislation—United States.
2. Nurses—Malpractice—United States.   I. Nichols,
Thomas S., 1934-   .   II. Hanson, Rachel,
1916-   .   III. Title.   [DNLM: 1. Jurisprudence—
United States.   2. Legislation, Nursing—United
States.   3. Malpractice.   4. Nursing—United States.
WY 33 AA1 M9L]
KF2915.N8M87   1982   344.73′0414   81-16956
ISBN 0-8016-3604-3   347.304414   AACR2

C/D/D   9   8   7   6   5   4   3   2   1   03/A/365

To
THE PATIENT

whose care is central to the health professions
and
whose safety rests in their hands

Preface

Since the first edition of *Legal Accountability in the Nursing Process* was published, the pace of changes in professional nursing practice has quickened. Public demand for increased health care and the ever-increasing scientific quantity and sophistication of knowledge and new technologies have continued their influences on professional nurses to accept even greater responsibility in independent practices. Therefore, it has become even clearer that, to accommodate the changes and demands, professional nursing practice must rest on a highly developed base of physical, biologic, and social sciences, to give the legal support necessary to bring into alignment the planning and implementation of health care.

Like the first edition, this revised work is based on the premise that law is a positive force and an essential component of the delivery of health care. The overall approach seeks to integrate law into the nursing process and thereby to lend support to independent practice. The power of the law to define nursing conduct is illustrated throughout the book, both in statutory law and in the case materials of tort law.

Recent litigated cases appear throughout the book to illustrate the level of practice for which professional nurses are being held accountable. Actual instances of a court's analysis of nursing conduct are reviewed against the background of a series of hypothetical situations, and the nurse is challenged to focus on the legal concepts relevant to current nursing practice.

The text opens with a proposal for enlarging the nursing process by the use of legal variables that enter into the formulation of a nursing plan and that can influence the outcome of nursing action. The book retains the format of the first edition and, following the Introduction, it is again arranged in sections that relate the law to four different frames of reference.

Section one, ''The Legal Boundaries of Nursing Conduct,'' has been revised to reflect recent changes in statutory law governing nursing practice and to provide a deeper understanding of the role of nurse practice acts in regulating health care. A summary of definition of nursing practice is discussed to show the extension of the scope of nursing functions. The section on voluntary controls has been expanded to show the power of professional organizations to determine their standards and to implement these standards through peer review and disciplinary action. Voluntary controls are considered both as standing alone and as forerunners to changes in statutory law and any untoward effects that may have occurred or are potentially liable to occur.

The chapter on disciplinary action has been restructured to explain in more depth how boards of nursing use legal authority granted in nurse practice acts to deal with derelict conduct. Two recent court-tested decisions of boards of nursing are reviewed and their process through the courts is examined.

Section two, ''The Reasonably Prudent Nurse,'' focuses more directly on the conduct of the individual nurse and demonstrates how knowledge of the law contributes to quality nursing care. A discussion of product liability is presented for the first time. Its purpose is to alert the professional nurse to legal considerations arising from the use of defective products.

A new chapter has been added on the professional nurse as a witness. The content distinguishes between factual testimony and testimony of an expert witness. The need for objective evaluation of the conduct of peers and the need to state it in a language understandable by the court are features of expert testimony that are treated. Recent litigation supporting the professional nurse as an expert witness is reviewed.

Section three, ''The Rights of Patients in Health Care Facilities,'' considers directly the patient's rights and applies the law governing nursing conduct in instances in which the fundamental rights of those who seek health care are at risk. The protection the law affords for the rights of patients is considered from the point of view of the professional nurse, who must take into account disclosure obligations and patient consent as a basis for any therapeutic action. The rights of the mentally ill are brought into sharper focus.

In Section four, ''The Nursing Process Legally Revisited,'' a three-step procedure for case analysis is offered as a method for examining legal decisions. The nurse is invited to follow how law ties its judgment to that of nursing by looking to the profession for a standard of care and how it imposes liability when that standard has not been met. Two recently litigated cases are presented (abbreviated but still detailed). The cases were selected as illustrations of current areas of professional nursing practice. They show use of a knowledge base to guide conduct, the independent nature of practice, and the interplay of working relationships that are a day-to-day experience in giving quality nursing care.

Designed for professional nurses, novices, educators, nursing service personnel, and experienced practitioners, the book is structured to stimulate a productive way of thinking about the law and its relationship to professional nursing. As a behaviorally oriented science, legal knowledge falls naturally into the interdisciplinary base of nursing science. In offering its rationale for the ''Why'' of nursing conduct, law takes its place among the basic sciences that have contributed to the depth and scope of nursing theory. Only when this related knowledge is synthesized into nursing science can it be used to improve nursing practice. Only if nurses understand the law will they be able to utilize it to direct their practice. Therefore, a professional nurse's knowledge of the law cannot stand outside the theoretical frame of reference but must become an integral part of all nursing theory and practice.

For this second edition, we wish to express our sincere appreciation for the professional counsel of Ann Bullock, Clinical Specialist, Psychiatric Nurse Practitioner; Deedy Buric, Assistant Clinic Administrator, Kaiser Foundation Health Plan of Colorado; Constance Drumheller, Associate Professor of Nursing, Loretto Heights College; Ann Gough, Executive Secretary, Colorado State Board of Nursing; Patti Whatley, Clinic Administrator, Kaiser Foundation Health Plan of Colorado; and Janet M. Velazquez, Instructor, Biological Science, Community College of Denver. We also wish to acknowledge the valuable assistance of Kathleen L. Ciborek, Ellen Edmunds, Pamela K. Lewis, Larry Harris, and Mary McPhee of the staff of Davis, Graham & Stubbs.

Irene Murchison
Thomas S. Nichols
Rachel Hanson

Contents

Introduction, 1

Professional nursing: autonomy—authority—accountability, 1
The nursing process—a proposal for its expansion, 3
An exercise in incorporating law into the nursing process, 6
  A medical regimen is questioned, 6

Section one

THE LEGAL BOUNDARIES FOR NURSING CONDUCT

1 Nursing and consumers of nursing share in its control, 13

Voluntary controls, 14
Historical development of legal controls, 17
The nurse practice act—a product of professional and legislative effort, 19
Legal control for nursing practice in the State of X, 20
  Preamble to the Nurse Practice Act, 20
  Definition of professional nursing practice, 21
Legal control for medical practice in the State of X, 22
  Preamble to the Medical Practice Act, 23
  Definition of medical practice, 23
Overlapping functions, 24
The nursing practitioner looks at nursing law, 25
  Society benefits by skilled nursing, 25
  The long arm of medical direction, 28
  Is it nursing or not? 30
  Summary, 32

2 Legal grounds for disciplinary action, 33

Legal review for disciplinary action, 34
Judicial review of a board decision, 35

Leib v. Board of Examiners for Nursing of State of Connecticut, 35
Tuma v. Board of Nursing, State of Idaho, 36
Grounds for disciplinary action in the State of X, 38
Board action to safeguard nursing care, 39
Reprimand for failure to supervise nursing personnel, 39
Suspension for gross failure to utilize available knowledge, 41
Revocation—the last resort, 43
Summary, 44

3 The common law, 45

Scope and meaning of the common law, 46
Early origins of tort law, 47
The meaning of tort law, 47
Liability for torts, 48
Negligence or malpractice, 49
Precedent—a principle of the common law, 51
Precedent—a force in shaping nursing conduct, 52
Departure from precedent, 54
Gugino v. Harvard Community Health Plan, 55
Applebaum v. Board of Directors of Barton Memorial Hospital, 56
Nursing accountability based on the common law of torts, 56
The court speaks to nurses about nursing, 57
A tale of two patients, 58
Summary, 60

Section two
THE REASONABLY PRUDENT NURSE

4 Standard of care, 63

The reasonably prudent nurse, 64
American Nurses' Association standards for professional nursing practice, 65
Standard of care for the expanding nursing role, 65
Risk taking—a factor in health care, 66
The professional nurse—a knowledgeable risk taker, 68
The nursing process relies on standards of care, 69
Reasonable judgment or unreasonable risk? 69
Practice based on principle—reasonable nursing conduct? 71
Summary, 73

5 Legal duty, 74

Duty of affirmative action, 75
Duty to foresee harm and to eliminate risks, 76
Colleague relationships, 77
Foreseeability—the challenge to professional nursing, 78

Assessment—a necessary forerunner of foreseeability, 79
Nursing action that concealed nursing judgment, 80
Labeling of patients interferes with duty, 81
Summary, 82

6 Causation, 84

Proof of causation—relevant variables, 85
Fixing responsibilities in multiple causation, 86
Products liability, 87
Failure to warn, 89
Drug liability, 90
Nursing role in products liability, 92
Products liability—one factor in the total field of causal relationships, 93
Res ipsa loquitur, 94
When nursing action causes harm, 97
   The action of Nurse Bowers as a cause of injury, 97
   Diet, a substantial factor in the therapeutic regimen, 98
   The injury speaks of negligence, 100
   Product liability affects nursing care, 101
   Summary, 102

7 The professional nurse as a witness, 104

The nurse as witness to facts, 105
The expert witness, 106
The nurse as an expert witness, 107
The expert witness and future nursing practice, 109
   The expert nurse witness evaluates nursing care, 109

8 Employer-employee liability for negligent patient care, 114

Vicarious liability, 114
Direct or corporate liability, 115
Liability for student conduct in a clinical setting, 118
The distance between employer and employee—a risk factor in patient care, 119
   "Do the best you can" nursing, 119
   A failure that threatened patients' lives, 121
   Summary, 122

Section three

RIGHTS OF PATIENTS IN HEALTH CARE FACILITIES

9 The basic human right to be free of intrusion, 127

Meaning and scope of rights, 127
Intentional intrusion on another's rights, 131

The nature of rights in a health care setting, 132
Nursing's responsibility for observing patients' rights, 133
The rights of the mentally ill or incompetent, 134
Nursing duty versus patients' rights, 135
   A patient's refusal leads to intentional intrusion, 136
   Learning threatens to invade privacy, 137
   Patient conformity and restraint of freedom, 139
   When nursing knowledge was not enough to protect a patient's right, 141
   Summary, 142

10   The meaning and mythology of consent, 144
Legal relinquishment of individual rights in a health care setting, 144
Disclosure as the basis for consent, 146
Disclosure allows for patient involvement, 147
Limitations on disclosure, 148
Creating an environment for informed consent, 149
Who gives consent, 150
The use and misuse of consent forms, 150
Verbal consent, 151
Consent—the priority of its position in the plan of care, 152
   Silence that was not consent, 152
   When consent becomes a ritual, 154
   Summary, 155

Section four
THE NURSING PROCESS LEGALLY REVISITED

11   Nursing conduct legally examined, 158
Delicata v. Bourlesses, 159
   Examining a fact pattern in a litigated case, 163
   Identifying the legal principles used in the judicial reasoning, 165
   Analyzing the nursing conduct to which the legal principles
      applied, 166
*Mirhosseiny v. Board of Supervisors of Louisiana State University and
Agricultural and Mechanical College,* 168
   Examining the fact pattern, 171
   Identifying the legal principles used in the judicial decision, 171
   Analyzing nursing conduct to which the legal principles
      applied, 172
The case that never went to court, 173
   Mr. Job's arrest, 173

Analyzing the fact pattern, 174
Applying relevant legal principles, 174
Identifying accountability, 174

12   Accountability—the full-time partner of autonomy, 176

The myth of dependent functioning in professional nursing, 177
Sharing the accountability for nursing acts, 177
Accountability as a measure of liability, 179

References, 180

LEGAL ACCOUNTABILITY
IN THE NURSING PROCESS

Introduction

PROFESSIONAL NURSING: AUTONOMY—AUTHORITY— ACCOUNTABILITY

Early in the twentieth century a nucleus of nursing leaders, sharing a vision for the future, laid the foundation for today's nursing by focusing on the preparation for professional nursing practice. Today, as a result of that vision, nurses are prepared to function at a level commensurate with other health professionals. As they assume a key role in the delivery of health care, legal accountability for their conduct becomes a major concern. To the uninformed, this concern may pose a threat; to the informed it offers guidance in formulating a plan of nursing action and support for expansion of the nursing role.

At one time nurses were in secondary risk positions—they were considered judgment-proof. Few carried liability insurance and even fewer earned salaries that could support a judgment in malpractice litigation. If a patient claimed harm and filed a malpractice suit, the primary liability fell on the employing agency and/or physician, even though the conduct of the nurse may have been the alleged cause of harm.

Today, nursing is concerned with health and wellness in an ever-expanding health care system. Acting singly or in a peer-colleague relationship with others, professional nurses are continually striving to meet the growing health needs of the community they serve. As health care becomes more complex and professional nursing more autonomous, an extension of legal liability follows. The physician or employer can no longer protect the legal or financial destiny of the nurse. Simply stated, the role of the professional nurse has changed, in a pragmatic sense, from one of legal dependency to one of legal accountability.

Autonomy has not been imposed on nurses. The nurse probably could have remained safely within the protective shadow of medicine if such behavior had not been contrary to the very nature of nursing. From the beginning of modern nursing, the profession has struggled to gain stature, to build curricula that would provide the basis for autonomous practice, and to provide the means for continuing intellectual growth that would ensure the right and obligation of nurses to share in the expansion of health services. Today, the professional nurse demands the right to think and act responsibly and, in so doing, must and does stand ready to be held accountable.

Accountability for one's acts also implies accountability to oneself. Inherent in this belief is the nurse's right to all the knowledge and tools that will safeguard her rights and the rights of others. The practitioner who operates from a frame of reference that encompasses only personal and professional accountability is denied the guidance and protection that derives from a knowledge of legal accountability. Until all professional curricula and continuing education programs recognize the law as an essential component of nursing practice, the positive force of the law is missing from the decision-making process, and both nurse and patient are the losers.

The challenge that flows from the concepts of autonomy, authority, and accountability cannot be denied; nor can the professional nurse be denied the means to accept such a challenge. The first step is the commitment of the individual and the profession to the idea that *nurses are professionals, and, as such, they have no dependent functions.* Once this legal position is accepted, nursing then needs to approach the study of law with the same conviction and purpose evidenced in the study of other disciplines related to the development and expansion of nursing theory.

> For too long, the study of law has been limited to the search for answers to narrow questions of procedure, or to concern over who would assume responsibility if the conduct of the nurse should be the cause of harm. This kind of discussion has been interspersed with liberal amounts of "anecdotal law." Without legal reasoning to support the decision, the discussions have been of little service in acquainting nurses with sound legal concepts and, in fact, have been psychologically disturbing in the overemphasis on the punitive aspects of the law.[1]

Whether, in a nursing sense, a professional nurse functions as an "independent" or "dependent" practitioner is of little or no consequence in the eyes of the law. Therefore, any swirl of controversy about the meaning of these terms, about the administrative acceptability of activities termed "independent" or "dependent," or about the nurse acting in an autonomous way or not are not helpful in resolving legal liability in the event an accident occurs in the scope of a nurse's professional practice.

Nurses in all facets of their professional practice operate within a legal framework of the professional person. This framework requires adherence to a standard of care measured by specialized knowledge and skills and provides the fundamental basis for enabling nurses to practice their profession. It follows that their professional associates and colleagues, including physicians and hospital administrators, cannot by fiat or policy substitute their wishes for nursing behavior for proper nursing conduct. In every instance when a nurse's conduct comes under legal scrutiny, it will be measured against that of the professional nursing practitioner and not against hospital policy or doctors' orders standing alone.

This is not to suggest that hospital policy and physicians' orders are irrelevant to the performance of a nurse's duty, but they cannot substitute for the necessary educational background, the reasonable use of skill in providing nursing care, and the exercise of that informed judgment that is the hallmark of the professional nurse.

Analyzing independent and dependent nursing functions in these terms, it becomes apparent why these terms are not adopted by the law. They carry with them an implication that nurses operating dependently renounce to some degree their professional stature and responsibility. Nothing like this is the case. In performing *all* their functions, nurses act professionally.

THE NURSING PROCESS—A PROPOSAL FOR ITS EXPANSION

The nursing process was born out of the need for a logical orderly approach to nursing care. It offers a structure through which the nurse, acting within a given set of circumstances, identifies patient (or client) priorities and mobilizes available resources to provide optimum care. It is action-oriented, yet its most telling feature is judgment, for in professional practice there are no ready solutions to problems. There are no rule-of-thumb procedures available to ensure a proper response in all situations; there are few absolutes on which to rely and a multiplicity of variables to be sifted and weighed before action is taken. Decisions, then, must come from a synthesis of ideas, principles, and constructs derived from the interdisciplinary approach that characterizes all professional conduct.

One way of viewing the evolution of professional thought and action is illustrated in Fig. 1, which follows the nursing process from its initial assessment to the ultimate evaluation of the action that was taken. In assessment, nurses draw from a broadly based background to arrive at goals that consider patients' conditions, their environment, alternative courses of action, and calculated risks to be taken in making choices. From this analysis the plan most likely to maintain or restore patient equilibrium should emerge.

Nursing goals alone, however, are not sufficient in themselves to move nurses from assessment to action. These goals must be considered within the context of their relationship to other dimensions, namely, professional standards and traditions, institutional policies and procedures, and relevant statutory and common law. While these dimensions may appear peripheral to patient situations, in reality they often control nursing action and may engender far-reaching consequences for the nurse and the nursing profession. For example, nurses who adhere blindly to tradition and/or institutional policy may jeopardize both their patients' welfare and their own professional stature. Similarly, nurses who lack a knowledge of law may find themselves charged with failure to exercise reasonable care in following, without question, a prescribed medical regimen.

The evaluation of a patient's response to nursing action may also be multidimensional. In addition to evaluation by the nurse directly accountable for the act, the action and the response it provokes may be further scrutinized by the consumers of nursing, professional peer groups, the administrative hierarchy, and, on rare occasions, the courts. It must be appreciated that, in general, the primary purpose of any evaluation is to assess the quality of patient care that has been or is being given, with the idea of improving care rather than threatening or accusing the nurse. Although it cannot be denied that serious legal scrutiny of nursing conduct can set limits for professional practice, it is also important to recognize that court action can evaluate the status of nursing and establish a precedent for a hitherto undefined extension of the nursing role. The capability of the law to either extend or limit nursing action, under certain circumstances, demonstrates that knowledge of the law should, at all times, be an integral part of the nursing process. To view the law in isolation mini-

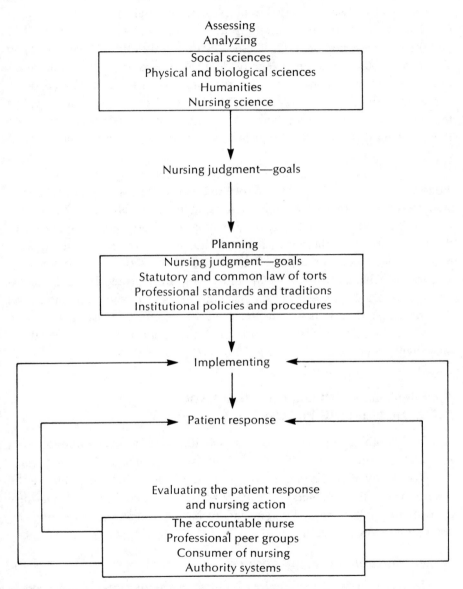

FIG. 1 Dimensions delineating the nursing process.

mizes its value as a resource for diminishing risk to both patient and nurse, and reduces its effectiveness as a tool for the improvement of patient care.

The legally aware nurse recognizes that, although risk taking is an inevitable part of high-level nursing practice, a knowledge of statutory law and the common law of torts, if used, can not only diminish risk but may also provide the basis for a legally defensible nursing decision. Furthermore, in determining when to take risks and when to set limits on one's actions and the actions of others, the professional practitioner must realize that in a situation of competing interests the law takes precedence even though it may run counter to institutional policies and professional standards and traditions.

In Fig. 1 the law was introduced into the nursing process at the decision-making level. Fig. 2 is now offered as a pattern for integrating substantive law throughout the entire nursing process. Nurses who have a knowledge of the law automatically include in assessment an appraisal of the legal variables inherent in a given situation. Furthermore, their judgments reflect recognition of the legal limits of the scope of their practice, and their decisions to act or withhold action are clarified by their understanding of legal duty and the standard of conduct by which nursing action will be measured. It is on the basis of the exercise of a legal duty to provide care and the expertise with which the action is carried out that the nurse will be judged.

AN EXERCISE IN INCORPORATING LAW INTO THE NURSING PROCESS

The hypothetical situation that follows illustrates a set of circumstances in which alternative courses of action must be weighed. It demonstrates the process by which a nurse used her knowledge, including that of the law, in a way that enabled her to respond positively to a professional duty in a relatively high-risk situation and to be comfortable in accepting accountability for her action.

A medical regimen is questioned

Memorial Hospital is a modern 300-bed private hospital in a metropolitan area in the state of X. Patricia Guise is the evening charge nurse on a 40-bed medical-surgical unit. About 4:00 P.M. Dr. Roman called to say that he was sending in a patient, Mrs. Yancey, a 70-year-old woman with

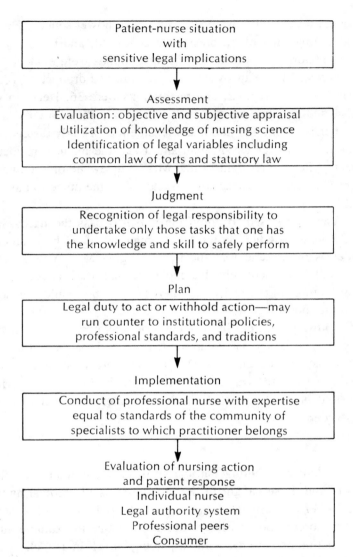

FIG. 2 Components for a legally defensible nursing action.

a tentative diagnosis of gastroenteritis. Dr. Roman stated that she had a history of mild coronary insufficiency but was not undergoing drug therapy. Until the present problem developed, she had been in good health.

One hour later Mrs. Yancey was admitted. Nurse Guise made a preliminary assessment and called Dr. Roman to report that the patient complained of nausea and cramping pain. She was vomiting frequently, and her abdomen was mildly distended with active bowel sounds. Her temperature was normal, her blood pressure was 120/80, and her pulse was 90. No cardiac abnormalities or abnormal lung sounds were evident.

At 6:00 P.M. Mrs. Yancey's blood pressure had dropped to 106/70, her pulse was 110 and irregular, and respirations were 36. Her skin was cool and moist, and her lips and nail beds were slightly cyanosed. Nausea and vomiting persisted and her abdomen became increasingly distended. Nurse Guise placed a call for Dr. Roman and asked the medical resident to see the patient. After the resident visited Mrs. Yancey, he ordered nasogastric decompression and electrocardiogram and asked the nurse to have Dr. Roman call him.

Mrs. Yancey refused to allow the nurse to pass the nasogastric tube until Dr. Roman saw her. When Dr. Roman called in, he countermanded the resident's orders and told the nurse to give Mrs. Yancey 10 mg of morphine sulfate immediately. He explained that Mrs. Yancey had had an electrocardiogram in his office recently; he said he would see her on his rounds in the morning.

Nurse Guise contacted the resident who was now actively involved in an emergency in the intensive care unit. He stated that he did not have the authority to act further and that Dr. Roman's orders should be followed. The nursing supervisor was called. Although she did not visit Mrs. Yancey, she told Nurse Guise that she had no alternative but to follow Dr. Roman's orders.

■　　■　　■

The problem confronting Patricia Guise is a common example of the dilemma of the nurse caught in the crosscurrents of medical and nursing practice. In her concern for Mrs. Yancey, Patricia was led to search beyond the customary boundaries of nursing practice to examine alternative courses of action open to her without placing herself in a legally vulnerable position. Continued careful examination of her actions and projection of possible further action will demonstrate the ease with which basic legal concepts can be integrated into the nursing process, and the way in which these concepts aid in determining responsible nursing action.

In her initial assessment, note that Patricia Guise, acting as a *reasonably prudent nurse,* took into account Mrs. Yancey's health history as well as the symptoms that had caused her to seek medical assistance. One hour later she was able *to forsee the potential for harm* in the continuing deterioration of her patient. Patricia was convinced that since Mrs. Yancey's condition was worsening she had *a duty* to intervene in order to prevent further harm. Her judgment was validated by the medical resident, but the decision to initiate more aggressive therapy was thwarted by a recalcitrant patient and lack of concern on the part of the attending physician. Patricia recognized that, in refusing to accept the treatment prescribed by the resident, the patient was exercising her *right* to participate in the plan of care and that forcing the patient to submit to the passing of a nasogastric tube would *be a violation of that right* and could well be grounds for legal action. At the same time she questioned whether the patient's refusal arose from her failure to understand the gravity of the situation and/or her inability to make a rational decision because of her increasingly critical condition.

When the support of the resident was withdrawn, Patricia found herself in the position of either accepting the opinion of Dr. Roman or initiating action, which in all likelihood would run counter to generally accepted hospital policy and nursing tradition.

She reassessed her position in relation to her accountability to Mrs. Yancey and to Dr. Roman. She was convinced the patient was deteriorating—the increasing abdominal distention was inhibiting respiratory function, there was obvious evidence of oxygen deprivation, and continued vomiting would lead to fluid and electrolyte imbalance. The change in vital signs indicated a beginning failure of the body's ability to mobilize its resources to cope with the problem. Patricia was convinced that further delay in establishing treatment would be costly, if not fatal, to the patient. Although the order for morphine might promote rest and some relief, she was concerned that it might also enhance the abdominal distention and mask symptoms. She determined that the drug order and nursing measures, such as reassurance and positioning to facilitate respiration, would not measurably alter the progressive decline of the patient.

Patricia knew that it was the intent of the Nurse Practice Act of the State of X to fix standards of accountability for the quality of nursing care given and that, by definition, she was granted the authority to carry out autonomous nursing functions that included acts of assessment, diagnosis, and care in the maintenance or restoration of health. Furthermore, she was aware that these functions should be based on systematic data gathering, discerning judgment, and skill and should be directed toward the treatment of human responses to an actual or potential health problem. She was also secure in her knowledge that, through *precedent established by common law,* she had a duty to *act affirmatively* to provide an *acceptable standard of care* for her patient.

Convinced that she was not being an alarmist, Patricia weighed alternative courses of action that might be taken. She knew that she had the judgment and skill necessary to initiate such actions as the administration of oxygen and parenteral fluids that would help to stabilize the patient's condition. However, she also realized that the most appropriate intervention would be determined only after further diagnostic procedures had been performed. Rather than initiating any heroic measures without further medical evaluation, she elected to call Dr. Roman again and review the clinical findings, making clear to him that failure on his part to accept her evaluation would force her to seek other medical counsel from the hospital staff.

■   ■   ■

In the preceding situation, Patricia Guise represents every nurse who has learned to incorporate into the nursing process those elements of law that give direction to responsible nursing conduct. The circumstances that led to the problem are not uncommon, and they serve to illustrate the multiple factors that influence a nursing judgment and the action that follows. Italicized words introduce substantive law, which will be examined in greater depth in succeeding chapters.

THE LEGAL BOUNDARIES FOR NURSING CONDUCT

The legal boundaries for nursing conduct provide the framework within which all nurses can safely engage in the practice of their profession. Patricia Guise, whose conduct in one instance was described in the foregoing introduction, is no exception. She is one of many nurses whose philosophy of nursing is rooted in the belief that every individual has the right to health care and that as an active member of the health professions she has the authority as well as the responsibility to protect that right. She recognizes that as an autonomous person, capable of decision making involving the life and/or welfare of others, she must accept accountability for her actions. Whether such actions are taken in response to medical direction or whether they result from her assessment of a situation and her recognition of the need for nursing intervention does not affect her accountability.

As a nursing student, Patricia learned that patient care is not a casual happening. Rather it is a carefully planned activity often requiring contributions from a variety of health care specialists. Early in her nursing experience she accepted the nursing process as the most effective method for implementing optimum care. As she became involved in the rapidly expanding role of the professional nurse, she came to rely on the law as a supportive science in determining whether to act or withhold action in a given set of circumstances. Her knowledge of the law was gradually integrated into her thinking until it became one of the significant dimensions of the nursing process.

Patricia's concern for Mrs. Yancey grew out of the clinical assessment that convinced her that the patient's condition was rapidly deteriorating. As she moved from assessment to a nursing decision, Patricia considered not only her clinical appraisal of Mrs. Yancey but also the peripheral forces that influence the selection of a course of action. She was well aware of the policies and procedures drawn up by employees of Memorial Hospital and of the hierarchy of authority and traditions common to health care facilities. She was equally aware, however, of the authority granted to her and her nursing colleagues by legislative enactment, of the sanctions that could be imposed if her conduct failed to measure up to an accepted standard of care. She was also alert to the force of the precedent of previous decisions made by the courts in their appraisal of the conduct of health professionals in similar situations. To facilitate understanding of the extent to which the law determined the course of action taken by Patricia in this instance, the three chapters that follow explore the impact of statutory law and the common law of torts on the practice of professional nursing.

1

Nursing and consumers of nursing share in its control

When nurses think of a law that controls nursing conduct, they are prone to think of statutory law as it exists in a particular state. This was the field of legal control they became familiar with as students and later experienced as they met licensure requirements when they entered nursing practice. While this legal area may be somewhat amorphous in the early stages of their professional careers, it becomes more real when nurses are confronted with changes in the law that affect the scope of their practice. When any law touches one's daily life and work, one naturally questions why the government should exercise control over that particular area of conduct. When a new nursing law is proposed, the concerned nurse will not only ask why but will also ask who will be responsible for writing the law, for keeping it current and descriptive of nursing practice, and even for defending it if it comes under attack?

Two groups must be considered when thinking about the control of nursing practice—the profession being controlled and the public or consumer being served. Both are vitally concerned with health care as a basic human right. Neither has a prior right over the other; rather, under optimum conditions, it is a healthy collaborative interaction. If the public interest is to be served, the nursing profession must fix standards for the licensure of those who are competent and guard against the encroachment of those who are incompetent and inadequately prepared.

Why must the state inject itself into the practice of professional nursing? The profession itself is concerned with defining boundaries of practice, with policing its members, and in general with exercising voluntary controls aimed at safeguarding the quality of care. One reason for state control is that while voluntary controls are powerful and persuasive, statutory controls are mandatory and, as with all laws, carry penalties for disobedience. Each augments and contributes to the effective functioning of the other. Any system predicated on just one form of control might interfere with the balance between the interests of those served and those rendering the service.

Statutory law evolves slowly, is carefully deliberated, and, when passed, represents the collective wisdom of the public and the profession in the state in which it is enacted.

To change or rescind statutory law is likewise an involved process. Herein lies a strength and a liability—a strength in that the process does not yield to whim or to individual dissatisfaction; a liability in that the process may be allowed to lag and no longer reflect current professional practice. When the law fails to adjust to advances being made in nursing and medical science, it may lead to a narrow interpretation of the scope of nursing practice in those decisions made by the courts.

VOLUNTARY CONTROLS

> The professional association is an organization of practitioners who judge one another as professionally competent and who have banded together to perform a social function which they cannot perform in their separate capacities as individuals.[2]

Professional practitioners are concerned with both voluntary controls and legal controls of conduct. Voluntary standards are developed and implemented by each particular discipline; they are not mandatory but are used as guidelines for peer review. Legal standards are developed by legislative action controling conduct and are implemented by authority granted by the state to license and to impose sanctions. The nursing profession follows this pattern of dual controls.

In 1896, when American nurses first recognized the need to work together, they organized under the name of the Nurses' Associated Alumnae of the United States and Canada. Canadian nurses withdrew in 1908 to form their own organization. In 1911, the Associated Alumnae changed its name to the American Nurses' Association. The statement of purpose of the Associated Alumnae, made at the time of its organization in 1896, was substantively the same as the overall purpose of the American Nurses' Association as stated in the 1952 platform:

To foster high standards of nursing practice and to promote the welfare of nurses to the end that all people may have better nursing care.[3]

The American Nurses' Association continues to foster this purpose in its ongoing reassessment of the functions, standards, and qualifications of its members. In so doing, the profession is guided not only by its own assessment of health needs, but also by the public's expectations for the delivery of health care.

In fact, the professional organization for nursing is the energizing force for the determination of nursing standards, both voluntary and legal. It is responsible for keeping each of these forms of control current as the needs for health services expand and shift. It is generally accepted by the public that the index to the level of development of a profession can be judged by the way it addresses itself to the standards and conduct of its members.

Voluntary and legal controls serve a similar social purpose, that of providing quality health care and guarding against unsafe practice, but they are distinctly different in the way they are developed and implemented. Voluntary standards are promulgated and activated by the profession. They are flexible and can be easily changed to keep pace with current practice. Legal controls are usually initiated by the profession and follow the judicial process in being made into law.

Voluntary controls often serve as forerunners of legal controls. In a rapidly changing social structure the nursing profession is continually confronted with issues that affect the practice of nursing, the preparation for practice and the safeguards necessary to protect the consumers of nursing. Under the system of voluntary controls, these issues are open to debate on local, state, and national levels. Such discussion often leads to a consensus of thinking expressed in the form of resolutions, standards, or guidelines, which in turn leads to action that allows for professionally controlled change in nursing programs or practice. Subsequently, after a period of supervised trial and evaluation, these changes may be incorporated into the law governing nursing practice. This process is illustrated by the use of standards in the development of criteria for accreditation of schools of nursing by regulatory agencies.

Recently the profession has been giving considerable thought and direction to expanding the role of professional nursing. This effort has resulted from the need to preserve the unique character of nursing, while at the same time taking action that will meet the challenge of a growing need for health services. The profession not only guides the development of standards but also guards against accepting functions without due consideration for the necessary preparation of practitioners to carry out these functions. Evidence of this form of control is found in the interdisciplinary work of nurses' associations and medical societies. Voluntary committees have been formed, functions have been studied, and statements have been made concerning the knowledge and skill necessary to implement a certain function. As a result of this movement, some jurisdictions have authorized, through their nurse practice acts, the formation of such interdisciplinary committees. If the recommendations of these committees meet with the approval of the Board of Nursing, they may be incorporated into the Rules and Regulations of the Board and become legally accepted nursing practice. This kind of interprofessional cooperation is one of the ways nursing has enlarged the scope of its practice. In critical care areas, professional nurses are authorized to make sophisticated judgments in dealing with cardiopulmonary emergencies and to carry out such techniques as arterial puncture and endotracheal intubation. In continuing care clinics and long-term care facilities, nurses, as primary health care givers, are now engaged in health maintenance and in the management of patients with chronic disease.

Another example of collaborative action is the plan followed in some health care agencies for nursing and medicine to develop standard procedures and protocols to expand health services through enlarging nursing functions. Through such planning, nurses are free to use their expertise in carrying out such activities as planning and implementing an immunization program, performing developmental evaluations and screening tests, and managing common self-limiting illnesses and minor accidents. Both of these interdisciplinary means of defining nursing conduct give broad powers to the prepared nurse and, when properly developed, should survive legal challenge.

As any profession undergoes change, it is obligated to guard against relinquishing functions as a matter of expediency without due regard to quality of its practice. To lose by default is shortsighted and irresponsible, for it is axiomatic that what a profession gives up it seldom gets back. No profession should block change to protect its own interests. However, by allowing certain nursing functions to be siphoned into areas of specialized practice such as inhalation therapy or patient advocacy, nursing may have seriously limited the nurse's ability to initiate a total plan of care.

HISTORICAL DEVELOPMENT
OF LEGAL CONTROLS

Governmental regulation of nursing practice through legislative action and the controls of regulatory agencies has existed in the United States for more than 70 years. Although the federal government, during this time, has been committed to support and safeguard the health of the nation, the actual control of the practice of any occupational group has been delegated to the individual states.

The movement for the statutory control of nursing began in early 1900, and gradually the fifty states and the District of Columbia had adopted nurse practice acts. Other than stating minimal educational standards, early laws offered little control over the practice of nursing. They were essentially registration acts controlling the titles under which nurses worked. Practitioners who were not licensed were not in violation of the law regardless of the complexity of functions they might assume, providing they did not hold themselves to be "trained," "graduate," or "licensed" nurses. This free-lance type of nursing was soon recognized as a public disservice, and mandatory licensure became the primary goal for legal reform in all jurisdictions.

Mandatory licensure for any profession or occupation simply means that all who practice for hire in a particular field are required to have a license. To select those qualified for a license and to prevent encroachment of the unqualified, it becomes necessary to define the scope of practice in the field coming under control.

To facilitate mandatory licensure, the American Nurses' Association, in 1958, published a model Nurse Practice Act. The definition approved for professional nursing is as follows:

The practice of professional nursing means the performance for compensation of any acts in the observation, care and counsel of the ill, injured or infirm, or in the maintenance of health or prevention of illness of others, or in the supervision and teaching of other personnel, or the administration of medications and treatments, as prescribed by a licensed physician or dentist; requiring substantial specialized judgment and skill and based on knowledge and application of the principles of biological, physical and social science. *The foregoing shall not be deemed to include acts of diagnosis or prescription of therapeutic or corrective measures.*[4] (Italics added.)

In light of the subsequent development of nursing, this model definition is indeed a historical pronouncement. It indicated the vision that nursing leaders had concerning the scope of the "cure" and "care" functions of professional nursing. It was farseeing in its recognition of an interdisciplinary base for nursing judgments and skills. The requirement that judgment and skill be based on the ability to apply principles derived from the sciences was an innovative part of the definition. Moreover, it implies that as science advances and new knowledge becomes available, the nurse is expected to keep abreast of it.

The first part of the definition clearly regards the professional nurse as an independent practitioner in the performance of acts of observation, care, counsel, teaching, and supervision of others. Nothing bars her from performing these acts, even though they could also be viewed as medical acts. It appears the only limitation placed on independent nursing action in this definition is "the administration of medication and treatments as prescribed by a licensed physician or dentist."

Although the total scope of independent nursing activities was broadened, the American Nurses' Association was willing to include a disclaimer that prevented nurses from diagnosing or initiating any therapeutic or corrective measures. The reasons for this disclaimer are speculative. They range from a desire to promote autonomy for the nursing profession, thus safeguarding its practitioners from becoming pseudomedics, to, at the other end of the spectrum, a means of seeking security in claiming that the physician made all the decisions.

At the time the resolution was adopted, educational programs were moving rapidly to expand the base of knowledge, which would increase the depth and scope of nursing science, and nurses were capably doing assessments and making decisions that bordered on a medical diagnosis. In fact, it might be said that when the definition was published, the disclaimer was already outdated.

Although nursing has a long history of efforts to create legal standards for nursing practice, medicine was the first of the health fields to seek regulation; even before the twentieth century, medicine sought legislative enactments to control its practice. This enabled medicine to preempt control of the total health field. While nurses, dentists, psychologists, and other groups have assumed certain responsibilities, the expansion of their functions has been limited to avoid encroaching on the law of medical practice.

THE NURSE PRACTICE ACT—A PRODUCT OF PROFESSIONAL AND LEGISLATIVE EFFORT

The power of the profession of nursing to control its practice, by direct or indirect means, is a force not to be denied. However, in a legal sense, the profession and the state have a shared responsibility for the development of a nurse practice act. Both are concerned with the health, safety, and welfare of the public. Each has a unique contribution to make, and neither could function effectively without the other.

Nursing has long been a victim of internal dissension, which has made the profession easy prey to external forces that may find it expedient to limit the extent to which the profession controls its practice. Any proposal to change the law that governs nursing practice is almost certain to provoke controversy within and outside the profession. This is understandable when one reflects on the complexity of the health care system. A change in the preparation or functions of any health care practitioner will not only affect those within the profession but will touch the practice of colleagues in related fields, the administration of health care facilities, and, ultimately, the consumer. Such intergroup strife and crosscurrents can deter or weaken needed legislation. If the public is to be well served, opposition must be faced objectively. The nursing profession must be clear in its thinking and forceful in enunciating its goals.

Therefore, it is essential that nurses, through their professional association, be involved in drafting a law that controls their practice, in interpreting its purpose to the community it will serve, and in guiding its passage through the legislature to subsequent approval by the governor. Combined professional and legislative effort can result in a nurse practice act that is realistic for today yet permits flexibility for tomorrow.

For their own protection, all nurses should be knowledgeable concerning the law governing nursing in the state in which they practice. It is the legal instrument that defines, for that particular jurisdiction, what the functions of nursing shall be and sets standards for licensure, which grants a nurse the authority to carry out those functions. Furthermore, familiarity with trends in the revision of nurse practice acts in other jurisdictions is advisable, for it will alert nurses to changes they might experience in future nursing practice.

LEGAL CONTROL FOR NURSING PRACTICE IN THE STATE OF X

In drafting a law controlling practice, a profession often expresses the need for legal authority in a declaration or preamble. This philosophical statement delineates the nature of the particular area of conduct and its importance to society. When and if the total law is passed, this preamble amounts to a public statement recognizing the goals and social position of the profession. It also sets the tone for the definition of nursing practice and the remainder of the law.

The preamble of a nurse practice act and the definition for practice vary from state to state in the precise wording of the statute, yet there are also many commonalities in their content. To avoid narrowing the reader's attention to any one state, the following preamble and definition of nursing practice were drafted for the hypothetical State of X after a review of current statutes and those being contemplated.

Preamble to the Nurse Practice Act

The General Assembly declares it to be in the interest of public health, safety and welfare to enact laws regulating and controlling the practice of nursing to the end that the people shall be properly protected from unauthorized, unqualified and improper practice of nursing in this state. Further, it is the intent of the Legislature that the registered nurse be directly accountable and responsible to the individual consumer for the quality of nursing care rendered. The General Assembly recognizes that the level of expertise of persons engaged in the practice of professional nursing is changing and professional nurses are increasingly capable because of their knowledge, judgment and skill of practicing independently and in collaboration with other health care personnel.

The General Assembly also recognizes the existence of overlapping functions between physicians and professional nurses and authorizes a sharing of these functions within the organized health care system by providing for collaboration between physicians and professional nurses. Such organized health care systems include, but are not limited to, clinics, home health agencies, physicians' offices and public or community health services.

This preamble constitutes an explicit statutory recognition that medicine and nursing are not isolated fields but overlap in their functions. It encourages continued sharing and collaborative efforts between the two disciplines. In so doing, it recognizes nursing's potential for improving health care and imposes on both professions the obligation to act in unison in the interest of a more complete health service.

Whether a preamble takes an expanded or narrow view of nursing, it reflects the beliefs of the community within which it was framed, and the definition of practice that follows translates these beliefs into operational terms. The definition, then, becomes the most significant part of the law for the nurse practitioner and the public because it states in more precise language what the functions of nursing are and what its legal boundaries shall be.

Definition of professional nursing practice

The practice of professional nursing shall mean the performance for compensation of acts requiring substantial specialized knowledge based on principles of biological, physical, social and behavioral sciences and which encompass autonomous nursing functions and delegated medical functions, both of which may be performed independently or in collaboration with other health team members or may be delegated by the professional nurse to other nursing personnel.

Such practice shall include the performance of any act in the assessment, diagnosis, care and counseling of persons in the maintenance or restoration of health and the prevention of illness. These acts shall be based on systematic data gathering, discriminating judgment and skill, and shall be directed toward the treatment of human responses to actual or potential health problems through such services as case finding, health teaching, health counseling and care supportive to life and well-being.

In the delivery of health care, professional nursing will share in executing medical regimens prescribed by a licensed or otherwise legally authorized physician or dentist and will establish nursing regimens which shall be consistent with, but shall not vary from, any existing medical regimen.

As used within this Act, unless otherwise indicated within the text:

    (a) "Diagnosing" shall mean the identification of, and discrimination between, physical and psychosocial signs and symptoms to determine whether a condition exists for which nursing care is indicated or for which referral to appropriate medical or community resources is needed;

    (b) "Treatment" shall mean the selection and performance of nursing measures essential to the management of a nursing and/or medical regimen;

    (c) "Human responses" shall mean those signs, symptoms and processes that denote the individual's reaction to actual or potential health problems;

    (d) "Case finding" shall mean the use of assessment and diagnostic skills to reach a conclusion that a condition exists for which nursing care is indicated or for which a referral should be made to another health professional or community agency;

    (e) "Medical regimen" shall mean that aspect of care that implements the medical plan as prescribed by a licensed physician or dentist;

    (f) "Nursing regimen" shall mean a systematic therapeutic plan designed by nursing personnel to carry out the practice of nursing.

As seen in these sections of the law governing professional nursing practice in the State of X, professional nursing continues to broaden its statutory basis for practice. This hyopthetical law is explicit in defining independent nursing functions while, at the same time, it retains those functions delegated by the physician or dentist. This change reflects a growing public trust and legislative confidence in professional nursing. It indicates that the professional nurse today must have a broader educational base and be prepared clinically to be perceptive in discerning variations from the normal range of human response in assessment and diagnosis.

While it is true that in the past nurses have often assessed patient needs and made professional diagnoses in carrying out the nursing role, the act of diagnosing was not generally considered, by either nursing or medicine, to be within the realm of nursing practice. In order for nursing to assume its share of responsibility in the health care system today, statutory definitions for nursing practice must give clear legal authority for an expanded nursing role and be less subservient in the language used.

LEGAL CONTROL FOR MEDICAL PRACTICE IN THE STATE OF X

As is true of nurse practice acts, the content of medical practice acts varies from state to state; however, many commonalities do exist. The preamble and definition for medical practice in the hypothetical State of X cited below were drawn up, after a review of medical practice statutes, to illustrate legal boundaries within which physicians practice. Their inclusion in this text provides the reader with an opportunity to compare and contrast the legally defined roles of physicians and professional nurses.

Preamble to the Medical Practice Act

It is recognized that the practice of the healing arts is a privilege granted by legislative authority and is not a natural right of individuals. It is therefore deemed necessary as a matter of policy in the interests of public health, safety and welfare to enact laws regulating and controlling the practice of the healing arts to the end that the people shall be properly protected against unauthorized, unqualified and improper practice of the healing arts in this state, and this article shall be construed in conformity with this declaration of purpose.

Definition of medical practice

The practice of medicine means: (a) holding out one's self to the public within this state as being able to diagnose, treat, prescribe for, palliate or prevent any human disease, ailment, pain, injury, deformity, or physical or mental condition, whether by the use of drugs, surgery, manipulation, or any physical, mechanical or other means whatsoever; (b) recommending, prescribing, or administering any form of treatment, operation, or healing for the intended palliation, relief, or cure of any physical or mental disease, ailment, injury, condition, or defect of any person with the intention of receiving therefor, either directly or indirectly, any fee, gift, or compensation whatsoever; (c) using the title M.D. or any word or abbreviation to indicate or induce others to believe that one is engaged in the diagnosis or treatment of persons afflicted with disease, injury or defect of body or mind, except as otherwise expressly permitted by the laws of the State of X enacted relative to the practice of any limited field of the healing arts.

Nothing in this section shall be construed as applying to osteopath, chiropractor, podiatrist, naturopath, optometrist, psychologist, nurse, dentist, or midwife duly and legally licensed by their respective state boards, when practicing their profession within the purview of the statutes applicable to their respective professions.

From the number of practitioners excluded in this Act, and in the laws of other jurisdictions, it is apparent that most, if not all, of those excluded are engaged in daily acts of diagnosis and treatment to relieve mental and physical conditions. Why then is the issue of the professional nurse being authorized to diagnose and treat looked upon by many as an infringement on the practice of medicine? Neither of these functions falls within the sole jurisdiction of either the physician or the nurse. The legal position should be clear. If either the physician or nurse uses the knowledge and skill that

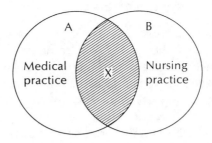

FIG. 3   Overlapping boundaries in nursing and medical practice.

he should have and practices within the category in which he is licensed, the health and welfare of the public are properly protected and there need be no concern for terminology.

It is possible that the interdependent relationship that characterizes nursing and medical practice and the extension of nursing into areas formerly considered to be exclusively medical practice have caused the conflict in legal definitions—which often use similar terms—to be unduly emphasized. Medicine and nursing have long traveled parallel roads without being fully committed to the premise that health service is built on interdependent functioning. To focus on the exclusive right of one professional group to carry out a specific function as basic to health care as the right to diagnose or treat could interfere with the ability of all health professionals to meet the growing needs of the public for health care.

OVERLAPPING FUNCTIONS

In many instances, an identical function might be considered the practice of medicine if performed by a physician and the practice of nursing if performed by a professional nurse. Therefore, instead of attempting to distinguish between a nursing diagnosis versus a medical diagnosis, it might be more legally accurate to consider the broad field of diagnosis in terms of a diagnosis by a nurse and a diagnosis by a physician.

The overlap between the professions is illustrated diagrammatically in Fig. 3, which indicates a gray area of overlapping boundaries in nursing and medical practice and in the statutory provisions for practice. Does this overlap mean that a practitioner in *A* or *B* may perform any or all of those functions that fall in the area of *X*? Hall, in a survey of the scope of nursing practice, states:

There is no reason why the traditional medicine/nursing dichotomy should be retained where it is no longer realistic. Therefore, except where political realities dictate otherwise, it should be discarded entirely and, optimally, be replaced by explicit recognition of the overlap of the independent practice of the professions of nursing and medicine.[5]

The problem of overlapping functions needs in-depth, objective study by nursing and medicine, not primarily to resolve the conflict of interest between the two professions but to provide a better service to the public. An optimal health care system needs qualified people to meet the growing health needs of a community, and that should be the base from which the question of overlapping functions is resolved.

THE NURSING PRACTITIONER LOOKS AT NURSING LAW

A knowledge of the statutory law regulating the practice of professional nursing within a given jurisdiction is necessary to enable nurses to compare their conduct objectively with the functions defined in the law and, in so doing, decide whether their practice complies with the law.

In the hypothetical situations that follow, the actions of certain nurse practitioners will be examined to determine whether their conduct falls within the legal definition of nursing in the hypothetical State of X. This exercise does not attempt to present a legal defense for the conduct of the nurse, nor does it presume to predict the outcome had the nurse's conduct been challenged in a court of law. Rather, it is suggested as an approach by which nurses can become more secure in their practice through an increased understanding of the legal boundaries of their profession. Analysis of the nurse's conduct in each instance should reinforce the reader's awareness that the scope of nursing practice is legally tied to the knowledge base from which professional judgment and action emerge.

Society benefits by skilled nursing

FACTS. Sadie Dickinson, R.N., is employed by a group of physicians in a large metropolitan area. Her primary responsibility is to conduct the admission assessment of all patients of the physicians' group. The goal of this physicians' group is to provide high-quality patient care through preventive medicine. Sadie enjoys her job, as it allows her independent decision making in her nursing practice. Using her nursing knowledge, judgment, and experience, Sadie conducts an in-depth appraisal, and arrives at a diagnosis of the patient's general health. She then refers the patient to the physician for follow-up care.

On Tuesday, Sadie's first patient was Dimitri Barbaros, who made an appointment at his wife's insistence. Mrs. Barbaros stated that her husband was "tired and run-down," although Mr. Barbaros maintained his fatigue was a result of depression from his work conditions.

During the interview, Mr. Barbaros revealed the following facts relating to his medical history: both his parents had lived in Greece and were now deceased, his father of unknown causes and his mother of a vague blood dyscrasia. Having had no serious illnesses or operations, he was apparently healthy until 3 to 4 months ago when he began to feel tired, weak, and depressed. He denied anorexia, weight loss, or changes in bowel habits. His stated occupation was a factory worker.

Physical findings revealed a 34-year-old, well-developed male with dark hair and pale complexion. There was no pallor of the mucous membranes and no lymphadenopathy. Abdominal examination revealed slight splenomegaly; rectal examination was normal; hematocrit and hemoglobin levels were within normal limits. The rest of the physical examination was unremarkable. Sadie then ordered the following tests: chest x-ray and electrocardiogram, urinalysis, complete blood count with indices, and SMA-7 (sequential multiple analyzer). Her impression was of a normal physical examination, although she felt it necessary to rule out tuberculosis, diabetes, liver disease, and anemia. Sadie discharged Mr. Barbaros, making plans to call him the following week with the test results.

The next week, after receiving the test results, Sadie was able to complete her data base. All reports were within normal limits with the exception of the blood report. The blood smear showed an abnormal shape of red blood cells and low blood indices. The hematocrit and hemoglobin levels were slightly below the accepted norms.

After reviewing and evaluating these data, Sadie's nursing diagnosis was minor thalassemia. Mr. Barbaros was referred to his physician for confirmation of the diagnosis and medical management.

ANALYSIS. Sadie Dickinson, R.N., has chosen to accept a position wherein her primary responsibility is to conduct physical examinations on adult patients. If, in the course of the examination, abnormal findings are elicited, Ms. Dickinson does not merely refer the patient to a physician for diagnosis. Instead, she expands her data base, arrives at a diagnosis, and then makes a referral to a physician.

In so doing, has Ms. Dickinson violated the Medical Practice Act of the State of X by carrying out a function specifically cited in that Act? One can pursue this point further by questioning whether the right and responsibility to diagnose is the exclusive function of the medical profession. If diagnosis is taken to mean critical scrutiny with its resulting judgment, it is hardly plausible that any knowledgeable person could carry out case finding, health counseling, or the initiation of health care without diagnosing. If the definition is limited to recognizing a disease from its symptoms, then it becomes more certainly tied to medical practice, but not necessarily to the exclusion of all other professionally prepared health practitioners.

It is important generally to recognize that a knowledge of the legal definition of medical practice is basic to understanding the relationship of medicine to nursing. However, a more useful direction to take in exploring the legal implications of Ms. Dickinson's professional conduct is to analyze her actions within the context of the Nurse Practice Act in the State of X. In the service she has provided for Mr. Barbaros, Ms. Dickinson has been chiefly concerned with acts of "assessment" and "diagnosis," both of which are designated in our hypothetical Nurse Practice Act as nursing functions. A review of this incident indicates that Ms. Dickinson's conduct complied with the law in that it was based on "systematic data gathering, discriminating judgment and skill" and was "directed toward the treatment of human responses to an actual or potential health problem."

The law further clarified the nursing role by defining "diagnosis" as "the identification of, and discrimination between, physical and psychosocial signs and symptoms to determine whether a condition exists for which nursing care is indicated or for which a referral to appropriate medical or community resource is needed." Arriving at a diagnosis of minor thalassemia, Ms. Dickinson elected to refer her client to a physician for treatment since she was aware that this condition was not one that would respond to nursing measures alone. Had she terminated her services to Mr. Barbaros at the conclusion of the admission assessment in order to avoid making a diagnosis, she would have failed to carry out a series of tasks necessary for the exercise of professional judgment, which is required by law in the State of X.

Sadie Dickinson's ability to diagnose is demonstrated in this situation. It is safe to say that not only did she identify and discriminate between physical and psychologic signs and symptoms, but she drew from her broad knowledge base to put disparate findings into meaningful wholes. She recognized that one or more conditions could be responsible for the patient's feelings of weakness and depression and laid out a plan sufficiently comprehensive to rule out or verify the presence of certain disease entities. It was at the point at which she intellectually linked the patient's Mediterranean heritage to the slight enlargement of the spleen that the working diagnosis of minor thalassemia was conceived, and the future health and well-being of Mr. Barbaros were made more secure.

If the primary purpose of the law defining any professional practice is to protect the public interest, it would seem reasonable that the law should conclude that the act of diagnosing can rightfully be a function of professional nursing.

The long arm of medical direction

FACTS. Hedwig Olms has had an interesting and varied career embracing both hospital and community nursing. Continuing education has been an integral part of nursing for Hedwig, and last year she completed a university program for advanced nurse practitioners, earning credentials that enabled her to expand the scope of her nursing practice. Shortly after completing this program, Ms. Olms accepted a position in a clinic located in an isolated farming community. The clinic had grown as a result of the needs and efforts of local residents, who had for years searched unsuccessfully for a physician to locate in their community. Failing this, they sought the services of a nurse who would work under the direction of Dr. Jarvis, who practiced in Elmwood, a community 150 miles away. Dr. Jarvis agreed to visit the clinic twice a month.

One of Ms. Olms' first patients was a farmer, Albert James. He was brought into the clinic complaining of extreme thirst, profound weakness, nausea, and visual disturbances. After a preliminary assessment that included a physical examination, health history, and laboratory tests available in the clinic, Ms. Olms diagnosed impending diabetic acidosis and immediately made arrangements to transfer Mr. James to the Elmwood Hospital. After a thorough workup under the direction of Dr. Jarvis, a diabetic regimen was initiated. Three weeks later Mr. James was discharged on a program based on dietary modification and insulin administration.

Ten days after discharge Mr. James again came to the clinic; he said that since he had gone back to work he had experienced general weakness and unusual sweating. Ms. Olms carefully interviewed Mr. James to elicit a more precise relationship of his symptoms to insulin, food intake, and activity. The interview, coupled with laboratory findings, led her to reduce the number of units of insulin the patient was receiving. Mr. James was somewhat reluctant to alter the regimen ordered by the doctor, but after Ms. Olms explained the relationship of glucose metabolism to activity, he agreed to follow the nurse's advice regarding the insulin. In addition, he agreed to report daily by phone the presence or absence of signs and symptoms that would indicate inadequate control of his diabetic condition. Five days later Dr. Jarvis made a routine visit to the clinic. Together, the doctor and nurse discussed Mr. James' progress. The doctor concurred with Ms. Olms' decision to regulate the insulin and countersigned the order on the patient's clinic record.

ANALYSIS. Like Sadie Dickinson, Hedwig Olms has elected to expand the scope of her nursing practice to include assessment as a tool for translating patient responses into a clinical diagnosis. Furthermore, she has chosen to practice in a clinic whose medical director is based 150 miles away, a decision that places her in a position of considerable responsibility and risk.

In the preceding incident, Ms. Olms arrived at a working diagnosis of impending diabetic acidosis and immediately made a referral to the clinic physician. In so doing she engaged in both case finding and initiation of health care, functions identified in the legal definition of nursing. Since she used her assessment skills to determine that a condition existed for which a medical referral was necessary, her conduct fell within the legal definition for nursing practice in the State of X.

On Mr. James' second visit to the clinic, Ms. Olms assessed his response to the medical regimen prescribed by Dr. Jarvis. Her decision to alter the dosage of insulin was founded on her knowledge of the relationship of physical activity to the body's ability to metabolize glucose. She was convinced that Mr. James was consistently experiencing symptoms of excessive insulin dosage and that, if adjustments in the medical regimen were not made, a hypoglycemic reaction could seriously threaten her patient's safety and well-being. In Ms. Olms' opinion, the most acceptable approach to treatment at this point was to reduce Mr. James' insulin intake and carefully monitor further responses.

The question now becomes whether the reduction of the insulin dosage is within the province of the nurse or whether it violated the Nurse Practice Act. To sanction Ms. Olms' decision as being within the definition of nursing practice would require one to interpret the act of altering the dosage of a drug as a nursing measure "essential to the management of a nursing and/or medical regimen." However, if her decision is interpreted as "varying the medical regimen"—a course of action explicitly prohibited by the law—one must ask how could Ms. Olms have acted responsibly toward her patient and yet have kept her activity within the legal boundaries of the Nurse Practice Act. Had she increased the patient's caloric intake to cover the insulin dosage, could that too have been considered as "varying the medical regimen?"

The fact that Ms. Olms is fulfilling a significant community need for health care can in no way be construed to justify conduct that runs counter to the law. In accepting the responsibility for the health needs of the community, she must be constantly alert to alternative courses of action that would safeguard patient welfare without jeopardizing her right to practice professional nursing. In this instance rather than varying the medical regimen on her sole responsibility she might have: (1) recommended that the patient return to his physician for further evaluation; (2) consulted with the physician by telephone and gained his approval of her decision; or (3) prior to the incident, established with the physician protocols by which she could exercise judgment in carrying out certain medical regimens in which a variation in response might be expected.

Is it nursing or not?

FACTS. The patient, Bea, was a 50-year-old, tall, capable-appearing woman. The therapist, Nona, had worked at a variety of general nursing positions for 10 years and then earned a master's degree in psychiatric nursing. Subsequently, she had worked for 10 years as a group and individual therapist in both community and private psychiatric clinic settings. More recently she had been functioning as a private, independent nurse practitioner. She continued to utilize peer supervision in bimonthly multidiscipline seminars and regularly participated in clinical courses at the local university.

Initially self-referred for marital counseling, Bea had utilized once-a-week outpatient therapy to work through her feelings about her divorce. She had spent many hours going over her intensely ambivalent relationship with her widowed mother, her five grown children, and her 30 years of martyred marriage to their alcoholic father. She spoke frequently of having no desire to live.

In her original evaluation the nurse noted that Bea lacked anxiety tolerance, impulse control, and consistent sublimatory channels. Assessment of the suicide potential was the first priority. Nona began treatment with a crisis-oriented supportive approach aimed at reinforcing Bea's defense organization and building a working relationship to help her achieve a more adaptive pattern of living.

After many months of regular contact with Bea, Nona saw more clearly in her defense constellation a borderline personality organization. Nona's treatment approach became more confrontive and interpretive, the focus more specific, and the therapeutic situation more structured.

In the fortieth treatment hour Bea appeared severely disorganized and negative. She demanded that Nona hospitalize her, stating that she was too sick to be treated on an outpatient basis. Nona focused on Bea's unrealistic expectations. She reiterated that treatment would be on a outpatient basis and firmly stated that together they would examine Bea's anger and reflect on its implications and sources. This session marked the beginning of a consistent but stormy working through of Bea's pathologic defenses. Eventually her reality testing was increased, her ego states more integrated, and her ability to form and maintain gratifying relationships was achieved.

ANALYSIS. Unlike the two previously described practitioners, Nona does not practice in a colleague relationship with a physician; rather, she assumes full repsonsibility for diagnosing and treating those who come to her for care. An examination of the preceding incident should provide an answer as to whether Nona has extended her professional service beyond that which is permitted by law in the State of X.

In the initial assessment, Nona observed certain behaviors that caused her to initiate a nursing regimen directed toward reinforcing her client's defense organization and toward building a working relationship that would help Bea achieve a more adaptive pattern of living. In so doing she has begun the process of diagnosing and treating a human response to a health problem. She was able to synthesize considerable substantive specialized knowledge from the behavioral and social sciences. This was demonstrated in the fact that she came to recognize in Bea the characteristic defense constellation seen in borderline personality organization. With refinement of the diagnosis, she redefined her goals and redirected her nursing activity in a more structured regimen.

Nona's conduct in diagnosing her patient's illness is very close to and perhaps overlaps the practice of medicine. While she has identified need and discriminated between physical and psychosocial signs and symptoms essential to the effective management of a nursing regimen, she has also, without medical support, acted as the sole agent in diagnosing and administering treatment to cure a mental illness—a matter quite clearly within the definition of medical practice in the Medical Practice Act of the State of X. Since the same Act specifically excludes from licensing requirement those who render nursing service in the lawful discharge of their duty, and since the Nurse Practice Act clearly allows the diagnosis and treatment of human responses to health problems, it can be argued that Nona is practicing nursing that is supportive and restorative and, at least in the State of X, legal.

However, since Nona is pioneering in a role as an independent practitioner, a question might be raised in the event that the patient came to harm—for example, committed suicide because the suicide potential was underrated or suffered an aggravated illness because the diagnosis failed to take into consideration a physical problem that deserved paramount attention.

When patients are suffering from a form of mental illness, their ability to contribute to their own safety and security is diminished, and their ability to distinguish between physical and emotional distress is clouded. The situation calls for perceptive assessment and a high degree of care with respect to the safety of these patients, conduct that should be characteristic of all professional nursing.

Summary

The three preceding situations illustrate the conduct of nurses who have looked seriously at expanding nursing practice and have acted to provide far-reaching service to the public. At the same time they have used to the fullest the knowledge base on which the practice of nursing is built, and they have helped to create within the community an expanded health care system through the development of a collegial relationship among health professionals.

In so doing they have relied on a knowledge of the law that both protects the public from incompetent practice and provides the legal framework that allows those who serve the health needs of the public to utilize their skills freely and with confidence.

2

Legal grounds for disciplinary action

The board of nursing in each state that is given legal authority, by statute, to issue a license is also given the power to take it away when professional conduct is such that it poses a threat to the health, safety, or welfare of the public. Just as in its definition for practice the law states what a professional nurse may do, so in its provision for disciplinary action the law states what a nurse may not do. In both instances the authorization is in broad general terms and at times must be interpreted by the courts.

In the imposition of sanctions, the board has wide discretionary power to deal with violations of nursing conduct in order that it may fulfill its obligation to the public. It is axiomatic that room for professional error enlarges as the role of nursing expands in response to scientific advances and as the number of health workers for whom the nurse is responsible multiplies. Also, the problem of personal dereliction mounts as society becomes more complex and nurses are subjected to pressure from within themselves and from the environment in which they live and work. The nurse practice act in a given jurisdiction provides the machinery for dealing with deviations from acceptable conduct.

Ideally, the first step in dealing with derelict nursing conduct is voluntary peer review by an appropriate committee of the state nurses' professional organization. However, a peer review committee can take action only if the professional charged is a member of the organization. This review should supersede, or may even obviate, the necessity of a legal review by the board of nursing. An admonition by one's peers can have a very salutary effect in controlling future conduct.

If the peer review does not suffice or is not indicated, then the legal route is followed and the case of misconduct falls within the purview of the board of nursing. When just cause is shown, boards are given power to issue an admonition; to deny, revoke, suspend or refuse a license; to place a licensee on probation; or to otherwise discipline in accordance with stated legal authority. In the imposition of any of these disciplinary sanctions, the board is given by law a considerable discretionary latitude to deal with acts of incompetence and misfeasance by nurse practitioners. In the exercise of this authority, certain rules of law must be followed. The nurse practice act in every jurisdiction describes the legal steps to be followed by the board before a sanction can be imposed for deviant conduct. Prior to any formal action, the board must have a sworn complaint setting forth the nature of the misconduct.

Numerous complaints of misconduct are informally received by the board, but many of them never reach the stage of a hearing because of insufficient evidence or because the complainant is not willing to sign the charges. One particularly difficult type of complaint for the board to assess and to deal with, in fairness to all, is a report to the board that a nurse is exhibiting bizarre behavior that poses a potential threat of harm to others. The board must proceed with caution in its investigation in order to safeguard the rights of nurses, as well as those who may come under their care.

LEGAL REVIEW FOR DISCIPLINARY ACTION

When a health care agency, professional organization, or individual submits a signed complaint setting forth the charges, the board first studies the facts as they relate to the scope of the authority of the nurse practice act. This enables them to determine the type of action to be taken, or if any is warranted. A fundamental question in any charge of personal or professional dereliction is whether the nature of the conduct complained of renders the practitioner unfit or unsafe to practice professional nursing. Misconduct does not of itself necessarily mean that the nurse is not qualified to practice. Rumor or hearsay does not offer a basis of evidence for a charge of dereliction.

The value of a professional license to practice is well known to nurses, for without it they would not be able to earn a livelihood. The license is viewed by the courts in the same way as is personal property, and it may not be taken away without following due legal process.

The procedure for disciplinary action is initiated when the board has reasonable grounds to believe that a licensee under the board's jurisdiction has committed acts in violation of the law. The procedure followed by the board in considering disciplinary action and the grounds for an investigation of conduct are carefully set forth in the law. A hearing between the board and the nurse accused follows due process similar to that in a court. The nurse is notified of the charges signed and sworn to by the complainant, stating the factual substance of the complaint and the time and place for the hearing. The nurse may be represented by legal counsel, witnesses may be called, and every opportunity is given the nurse to offer a defense. If the board then reaches an informed judgment that the conduct of the nurse has failed to meet the requirements of statutory law, sanctions may be imposed. Even then the nurse is not without recourse, for final board action may be judicially reviewed by a court.

When a sanction is imposed by the board of nursing on an individual, and the individual believes an error has occurred, either in the analysis of the evidence or in the procedure followed by the board, the nurse has the right to challenge the decision by asking for a judicial review. A challenge is first filed in a lower court. The function of this court is to examine the legal authorization for the sanction imposed and decide if the board exercised its power with wise discretion, if it acted capriciously, or if it exceeded its authority. The court then has the power to either sustain the decision of the board or to rescind it on the grounds of the finding of fact or the procedure followed or both. When the court has acted, the nurse or the board has the right to appeal the decision to the state appellate courts.

JUDICIAL REVIEW OF A BOARD DECISION

Summaries of two recent decisions follow. They illustrate the way the courts deal with a challenge to action taken by the board of nursing in the imposition of sanctions.

Leib v. Board of Examiners for Nursing of State of Connecticut[6]

FACTS. Leib was charged with charting the administration of Demerol to a patient when, instead, she had converted it to her own use. Prior to the hearing conducted by the board, Leib voluntarily signed a statement admitting guilt to the charges and further admitted that on previous occasions she had followed this same practice. The board revoked her license on the grounds that her conduct failed to conform to accepted standards of professional practice.

JUDICIAL PROCESS. Leib appealed to the Common Court of Pleas in the State of Connecticut, stating that the findings of fact by the board of nursing and the decision went beyond the scope of the notice of the hearing sent to her. Therefore, she claimed that due process had not been followed. This court held that Leib's claim had no merit and dismissed the case. Leib then appealed to the state Supreme Court.

The Supreme Court sustained the decision of the board of nursing, which had stated that the immediate conduct of the nurse had violated standards of professional behavior. In this decision, the Supreme Court recognized the board of nursing as a body of qualified experts in the field being regulated. It held that, as such, the board had acted within its legal authority in evaluating professional conduct. The key to this decision was that the board was authorized to examine conduct in the light of the evidence of the individual case at hand.

Contrast the above with the case to follow, in which the Supreme Court in another state did not sustain the decision of the board in its finding of unprofessional conduct because the board had failed through its rules and regulations to define the statutory term that it had used as a basis for its authority for revocation.

Tuma v. Board of Nursing, State of Idaho[7]

FACTS. Tuma, a clinical instructor in a local college, supervised students in a hospital setting. In this capacity, she, together with a student, visited a terminally ill patient suffering from leukemia for whom chemotherapy had been ordered by her physician. The patient told Tuma that she had fought leukemia for 12 years and attributed her success to the practice of her religion. She had been told about the side effects of chemotherapy by her physician. Tuma and the patient discussed alternative treatments to chemotherapy, among them natural products and Laetrile. The student nurse later testified that Tuma had told her to forget what she heard because it was not "exactly legal." At the patient's request, Tuma met with her and her family to discuss alternative treatments. The patient asked the family not to tell the physician. However, a member of the family did so. The physician discontinued the order for chemotherapy because of the patient's change of attitude, but it was later reordered the same day.

The patient died within 2 weeks, and the subsequent legal review showed that the delay in the administration of chemotherapy had no significance.

JUDICIAL PROCESS. The board of nursing received sworn complaints from hospital personnel, stating that Tuma had interfered with physician-patient relationships. A hearing was held, and it was determined that Tuma had in fact discussed natural products as an alternative treatment to chemotherapy but had not stated they would cure the patient and, furthermore, that Tuma had said that the care of a ''reflexologist'' could be arranged if the patient decided to accept alternative treatment; the circumstantial evidence indicated that Tuma had offered to make the arrangements. The board, after a review of the evidence, suspended Tuma's license for 6 months for unprofessional conduct.

Tuma appealed the decision to the district court, asking for a new trial, which was denied. The district court then affirmed the order of the board, without opinion on Tuma's conduct. Tuma appealed the decision to the state Supreme Court.

The Supreme Court of Idaho reversed the decision of the board to suspend Tuma's license. It stated that, in the absence of a legislative or administrative definition of ''unprofessional conduct,'' the board had acted without due process.

ADDENDUM. It is significant to note that, in each of these cases, neither the lower nor the higher court evaluated the actual nursing conduct that was the basis of appeal. Many times, nurse readers misinterpret a legal decision to mean that the nurse was found guilty of misconduct or was exonerated. Actually, the case may have turned solely on a legal issue of procedure. ''Due process'' is an important legal concept, which requires that any judicial or administrative action leading to the imposition of penalties or sanctions must be carried out fairly, with a full opportunity being rendered to the person charged to defend himself. In the Leib case, the defendant held that due process had been violated because matters were considered at the hearing which had not been included in the notice of the charges sent to Leib. The courts did not support this position. The court made no comment on whether or not it found Leib's conduct to be unprofessional. In the Tuma case, many nurse readers would see Tuma's conduct as preempting the therapeutic plan of the physician and a violation of colleague relations with the physician. However, the court did not deal with Tuma's conduct, be it ethical or otherwise, but reversed the board's decision on the procedural ground of failing to follow due process in invoking the sanction.

GROUNDS FOR DISCIPLINARY ACTION IN THE STATE OF X

When the definition for professional nursing practice in the State of X was first presented in Chapter 1, it was stated that it did not follow the nurse practice act of any particular state; rather, it was a compilation made from numerous state laws. The analysis of the grounds for disciplinary action in the State of X continues in the same pattern and represents a composite of current and proposed law dealing with deviant nursing conduct.

The Board, by an affirmative vote of at least five of its nine members, shall have the power to deny, revoke or suspend any license to practice professional nursing issued or applied for in accordance with the provisions of the law of the State of X, or otherwise to discipline a licensee upon proof that the licensee:

1. Is guilty of fraud or deceit in procuring or attempting to procure such license
2. Has been convicted of a felony or misdemeanor involving moral turpitude or gross immorality
3. Is unfit or incompetent by reason of neligence or other causes
4. Is habitually intemperate or is addicted to the use of habit-forming drugs
5. Is mentally incompetent, physically or psychologically impaired
6. Is guilty of unprofessional conduct
   (1) Unprofessional conduct shall mean but not be limited to:
       (a) Inaccurate recording, falsifying or altering patient records
       (b) Administering medications and treatments prescribed for patients in a negligent manner
       (c) Performing acts beyond the limits of the practice of professional nursing
       (d) Failing to take appropriate action in safeguarding the patient from incompetent health care practice
       (e) Violating the confidentiality of information or knowledge concerning the patient
       (f) Conduct unbecoming a person licensed to practice professional nursing or detrimental to the public interest
       (g) Assuming duties and responsibilities in the practice of

professional nursing when competency has not been maintained

(h) Discriminating in the rendering of nursing services as it relates to human rights and dignity of the individual

(i) Willful violation of any provision of the Professional Nursing Practice Act

BOARD ACTION TO SAFEGUARD NURSING CARE

To assume that all professionals measure up to standards defined by the profession and/or by law is to deny the existence of human frailty. In fact, one of the criteria for a profession is that is shall ensure professional competence by action that sets limits on those who offer their services to the public. Written into nursing law are the standards and processes by which nursing conduct, brought to the attention of the board by the consumer or professional peers, shall be judged and acted on.

The following instances relate to conduct that in the judgment of the Board of Nursing of the State of X did not measure up to the standards cited in the Nurse Practice Act. In all three instances the Board, after inquiry and examination of the facts, assumed responsibility for safeguarding nursing practice by reprimanding and suspending or revoking the license of practitioners whose conduct had led to less than satisfactory patient care.

Reprimand for failure to supervise nursing personnel

FACTS. Jean Oswald, R.N., has been the evening charge nurse in the Emergency Room and Outpatient Department at Weaver Memorial Hospital for 4 years. Presently, her staff includes a nurse's aide and a licensed practical nurse, Sarah Johns. Mrs. Johns has been employed at Weaver Memorial Hospital for 14 months. She is an aggressive person, inclined to disregard hospital policy and regulations. Repeatedly, Ms. Oswald has counseled Mrs. Johns is relation to behavior that had gone beyond the limits of her preparation and job description in giving direct care or counsel to patients. Examples of this behavior ranged from checking a patient with an acute condition of the abdomen for rebound tenderness to examining a child's eardrums and recommending heat and aspirin to the child's mother. In spite of such incidents, Ms. Oswald gave Mrs. Johns a satisfactory rating on both her 6- and 12-month evaluations. She had, however, suggested to the evening supervisor that she believed Mrs. Johns would be a more productive employee in a work setting that was more routine and controlled.

At 4:00 P.M., on a quiet Monday, Mr. Sloviac was admitted to the emergency room with a laceration of the forearm. Within the hour he was seen by his physician, who cared for the wound and determined that the patient's condition did not require hospitalization. At 5:30 P.M., Ms. Oswald left the department for her supper break. Before leaving she advised Mrs. Johns that Mr. Sloviac was discharged and could leave as soon as his family called for him and that she would be in the hospital cafeteria should an emergency arise. On returning to the unit she noted that the cautery had been used. She questioned Mrs. Johns, who explained rather casually that Mr. Sloviac had asked her to remove several moles from his neck and that she had done so.

Realizing that she was unable to cope with Mrs. Johns' behavior and that this behavior posed a threat to patient welfare, Ms. Oswald took her problem to nursing service. After thoughtful deliberation by the nursing service staff, it was agreed that Mrs. Johns' conduct jeopardized patient safety and she should be discharged. It was also determined that Ms. Oswald had failed to provide adequate supervision and a notification to that effect should be sent to her. Furthermore, a signed complaint regarding the conduct of the two nurses was to be submitted to the Board of Nursing.

ANALYSIS. When the report from Weaver Memorial Hospital was reviewed by the Board of Nursing in the State of X, consideration was given to the conduct of both Mrs. Johns and Ms. Oswald. It was the consensus of the Board that, while not in any way condoning the behavior of the practical nurse, priority should be given to evaluating the role of the professional nurse in safeguarding patient welfare. As a result of their deliberations, Ms. Oswald was reprimanded for failing to deal positively with a member of her staff who had consistently jeopardized the welfare of emergency room clientele.

For some time Ms. Oswald had recognized Mrs. Johns' inappropriate behavior in carrying out techniques and making judgments that were well beyond the scope of her training and skill and that could have had serious consequences for patients. Although Ms. Oswald had brought this conduct to Mrs. Johns' attention, she had given her two satisfactory evaluations. Furthermore, although she had made a casual reference to Mrs. Johns' work to the evening supervisor, she had not offered data to support her judgment nor had she indicated the serious nature of Mrs. Johns' conduct. Consequently, no action was taken until Mrs. Johns carried out a procedure that was considered to be exclusively within the realm of medical practice.

It was determined by the Board that Ms. Oswald had failed to take appropriate action in safeguarding a patient from improper health care practice and had, over a period of a year, observed incompetent conduct without taking appropriate action within the agency to set limits that would have further prevented such conduct. In reprimanding Ms. Oswald, the Board emphasized that rarely can professional nursing be carried out in isolation and, as a result, it is the responsibility of all professionals not only to exercise a high degree of expertise in giving direct care but to coordinate and supervise the work of others, so that at all times the care provided will be supportive and restorative to life and well-being.

Suspension for gross failure to utilize available knowledge

FACTS. Clara Covert, R.N., had been employed as an office nurse for Dr. Gomez, a general practitioner, in a city of 250,000 population for 10 years. She was active in community affairs and nursing organizations and was well liked and respected by those who made up Dr. Gomez' practice.

On a Saturday morning in late May she was alone in the office while Dr. Gomez was attending an out-of-town medical meeting. Just before closing, a young mother, Mrs. Oliver, brought in her 10-year old son, Billy, who had a small puncture wound of the left heel. It was the Olivers' first visit to Dr. Gomez, and the mother was somewhat apprehensive to find that a physician was not in attendance. Ms. Covert assured Mrs. Oliver that the injury was not serious. She cleansed the wound and applied a sterile dressing. In the process she asked Mrs. Oliver two questions: "Has Billy been inoculated for tetanus?" "Does he have any known allergies to drugs?" Mrs. Oliver replied "yes" to the first question, "no" to the second. Nurse Covert administered a penicillin injection to Billy, telling Mrs. Oliver that such an injection was routine office procedure. Billy was discharged with the advice to return if any drainage, redness, or swelling at the puncture site was observed.

Early the following Friday, Dr. Gomez was called to the Oliver home. He found Billy in a semicomatose state; his breathing was stridulous, his head was retracted, feet fully extended, and back arched. His parents reported that for the last 2 days he had not been his usual self. Although somewhat lethargic, he had been unusually irritable. When he failed to appear for breakfast, Mrs. Oliver went to awaken him. She became alarmed when she noted his odd posture and noisy breathing. Attempts to arouse him initiated a generalized convulsion.

After a cursory history and examination, Billy was transported to the hospital. Therapy with large doses of tetanus antitoxin and sedative drugs was initiated. Billy recovered with no apparent sequelae. The parents, however, were convinced that proper initial treatment would have prevented Billy's illness. Although they had no desire to pursue a charge of malpractice against Ms. Covert, they felt compelled to register a formal complaint with the State Board of Nursing.

ANALYSIS. In analyzing the circumstances surrounding Billy Oliver's injury and subsequent illness, the Board of Nursing of the State of X was unanimous in its opinion that professional acts shall be based on systematic data gathering, discriminating judgment and skill, and shall be directed toward the treatment of human responses to actual or potential health problems through nursing care that is supportive and restorative to life and well-being.

In examining the evidence the Board concluded that Nurse Covert had failed to gather sufficient data on which to base her actions. More specifically, she did not find out when the patient had received tetanus toxoid and if, or when, a booster had been given. She did not inquire into the conditions under which the injury had occurred, an inquiry that, if made, would undoubtedly have led her to be more aware of the inherent danger of tetanus. Furthermore, she gave limited direction to Mrs. Oliver, focusing only on the wound and disregarding systemic response to injury. In short, Ms. Covert failed to use knowledge of biologic and medical sciences in formulating the judgment on which she based her actions. In addition, she demonstrated a lack of interviewing skill, which led to incompetence in dealing with Billy's immediate needs and in determining the proper focus for follow-up care.

It was also agreed that the administration of penicillin in this instance would not qualify as action taken to provide necessary support in a life-threatening situation; rather it reflected a predisposition on the part of Ms. Covert to unnecessarily blur accepted legal boundaries of medical and nursing practice.

It was the consensus of the Board that Ms. Covert had demonstrated incompetence in the practice of nursing, which exposed the patient to definite and immediate harm, and that her general conduct indicated a failure to keep current the knowledge and skills basic to the practice of one whose responsibility is that of providing primary health care. The decision of the Board was to suspend Ms. Covert's license and to require her participation in relevant continuing education programs before applying for reinstatement.

Revocation—the last resort

FACTS. For 7 years Abigail Noyes, R.N., had been working in the community of Galesburg. The length of her employment at any one institution had not exceeded 16 months. Her present position was at City Hospital, where she was night nurse on a thirty-bed surgical unit. During this period of employment, several incidents were reported to nursing service that could have resulted from inadvertence or lack of knowledge. The most serious incident involved an error in the intravenous administration of potassium.

Several weeks previous, at 2:30 P.M., an elderly gentleman, Mr. Klum, was admitted to Ms. Noyes' unit following emergency surgery for a bowel obstruction. His condition was critical and postoperative orders were numerous. One order directed the nurse to pass a nasogastric tube and maintain suction at low pressure.

During the night, the practical nurse assisting with Mr. Klum's care repeatedly reported that the tube was not draining and that Mr. Klum seemed to be having more difficulty breathing. Ms. Noyes suggested irrigating the tube and changing the suction from low to high pressure. She visited Mr. Klum twice—once to regulate the intravenous flow rate and at 6:00 A.M. when she assessed the patient's overall response during her final patient rounds.

At 6:30 A.M. Mr. Klum was visited by the surgical resident who, struck by the obvious deterioration of the patient, immediately initiated more aggressive therapy. A chest x-ray film revealed that the nasogastric tube had been passed into the left bronchus. The incident was reported to nursing service. Ms. Noyes was discharged and a complaint was filed with the board of nursing.

ANALYSIS. Confronted with the conduct of Ms. Noyes in the exercise of her duty to safeguard the welfare of Mr. Klum, the Board of Nursing of the State of X held that Ms. Noyes had demonstrated incompetence in her failure to use professional judgment and skill in executing a medical regimen and in establishing a nursing regimen that was supportive to life and well-being.

Her inability to recognize the improper placement of a nasogastric tube rested on failure to appreciate the risks involved and to utilize commonly accepted procedures for checking the placement of such a tube plus a total lack of appropriate supervision of a postoperative patient. Instructions given by Ms. Noyes to the practical nurse for the management of the tube were in direct violation of medical orders. Failure to provide reasonably frequent assessment of the patient's condition demonstrated both a lack of understanding of the potential for harm and little or no concern for an individual patient's welfare.

In determining the action to take relative to the conduct of Ms. Noyes, the Board summarized its findings and ruled that since the patient's safety and well-being were seriously jeopardized by imcompetent nursing practice for which Ms. Noyes was directly and indirectly responsible, and since her work record revealed a continuous failure to maintain a satisfactory level of practice, her license to practice professional nursing should be revoked.

Summary

In reflecting on the conduct of the three nurses who were found by the board in the State of X to be guilty of varying degrees of failure to practice at a satisfactory level, it becomes obvious that in each instance the nurse perceived her profession within a narrow range of functioning, failing to see beyond the immediacy of a nursing act or to assess the potential for harm in a given situation.

In all instances it is beyond question that a better understanding of the nature of nursing would have lessened the possibility of failure. But it is also quite likely that, had these nurses been schooled in the legal definition and control of nursing practice, they would have been better prepared to reach a nursing decision that would have more effectively served their patients' needs without threat to their right to function professionally.

3

The common law

Study of the social sciences encompasses much of the study of law in a general sense. All of the social requirements, taboos, and superstitions that exert their powerful influence on cultures, ancient and modern, arise from within the culture and carry with them sanctions for their disregard. Law, too, in this broad sense is a product of a continuing reworking of attitudes and ideas transmitted from one generation to the next. Law cannot exist apart from society or separate from social, political, and economic forces, from which springs the need for its very existence and which gives it life, force, and power.

Law is one means that society uses to control conduct. It is a form of command that can be viewed as a positive social force; as it defines acceptable conduct, it serves as a deterrent to other, unacceptable forms of conduct. However, it must be appreciated that no such thing as *the law* exists. There is no fixed system of rules that can be mechanically applied to reach results that are fair and just for everyone. Rather, law must be interpreted in relation to specific situations. It is sensitive and moves with social change; it reflects recognition and understanding of advances in social and scientific thought.

Law is a socially oriented discipline and, like nursing, is committed to the welfare of society. Together they share many societal similarities: (1) Each sees a state of wellness as a sought-for optimum condition for both the individual and the social group. (2) Each intervenes when there is an interruption in the state of wellness that is manifested by altered conduct. When this occurs, each takes steps to restore individual or social equilibrium. (3) Each turns to the social and behavioral sciences to understand conduct and to guide remedial action. While both are distinct disciplines, nursing can draw from law to broaden its theoretical base and strengthen its operation as a socially oriented discipline.

Law makes a contribution to professional nursing by defining rules of conduct that brings logic and authority to the decision-making process. As with other disciplines related to nursing, such as the physical and biologic sciences, law must also be synthesized into nursing science before it can be utilized to enhance the quality of nursing care.

America's system of law can be divided into statutory law and common law. As discussed in the foregoing chapter on nurse practice acts, statutory law is determined through the legislative process. Common law makes up all other legal rules of conduct on which the statutes are silent.

SCOPE AND MEANING OF THE COMMON LAW

The common law, of which tort law is a significant part, has evolved from hundreds of years of decisions made by the English and American courts. It is essentially judge-made law, which has developed through the resolution of innumerable disputes and controversies that have been brought to the attention of the courts.

The social scientist may see the common law simply as many instances of deviant conduct and the particular action that was taken to control individual conduct for the good of society. The attorney sees the common law as a total body of law in which the decision of one case rests upon and is related to others as the basis for a system that determines accountability. The attorney sees the common law as a composite of judicial decisions concerned with the protection of personal liberty, personal security, private property, and the protection and enforcement of various types of contracts.

> The common law has enormous influence upon the daily conduct of affairs and business. No statute says that contracts entered between individuals are enforceable; that is left to the common law. No statute says that the person who negligently harms another is responsible for the financial losses of the injured person; the common law does that. No statute says that a promissory note obtained by fraud and deceit is unenforceable; again, that is the function of the common law.[8]

A remedy of the common law, means by which a right is enforced, is essentially private in scope and character because it involves the settlement of a dispute between individuals. If a person feels that his rights have been trampled on, he must take the initiative, put the legal machinery in motion, and finance its operation to secure the type of relief that the common law offers.

EARLY ORIGINS OF TORT LAW

The evolution of the common law of torts is a running account of the conduct of humans throughout the ages. From earliest times humans have been in conflict with one another. Primitive people did not seek equity or justice in their acts of vengeance. If one put out the eye of another, the victim retaliated with conduct that might have been totally irrelevant to the assailant's act. As thinking changed, vengeance began to be limited to the eye-for-an-eye rule. It may be at this point that the judicial system had its beginning as tribal leaders developed procedures for determining the amount of revenge the victim was entitled to receive. Gradually a system of payment for damages was substituted for that of personal revenge. This change brought about the development of peacemaking courts, which, although not concerned with deciding facts and applying law, did exercise some degree of authority in maintaining order in the tribal community.

Under Old Testament law the idea of accountability for oneself and one's property began to emerge. For example, if an ox gored a man, the owner was not considered to be responsible if he did not know that his ox was dangerous. But "if the ox were wont to push with his horns in times past, and it hath been testified to his owner, and he hath not kept him in," the owner was held accountable. Here, in this ancient law, are the beginnings of the concept of negligence so important today to institutions and persons involved in the delivery of health care.[9] Down through the centuries men have continued to build from their common experiences a body of law that, although not set down explicitly in writing, has enabled communities of people to live together with some measure of fairness, consistency, and impartiality.

THE MEANING OF TORT LAW

Tort law is but one part of the body of common law and deals mainly with harm that may come to an individual either through inadvertence or intent on the part of another. The scope of tort law becomes more apparent when one understands that tort means conduct which is twisted or which is generally recognized as socially undesirable. The term is applied to a miscellaneous collection of civil wrongs, including assault, battery, false imprisonment, and negligence. A tort can be an action or an omission, either of which causes injury and which may result in a claim for compensation for damages suffered.

> The overriding objective of the tort law is to provide a means for compensating those injured by the wrongful conduct of another. It is not primarily designed to punish or penalize, although it may indirectly do so. It seeks, by awarding money damages, to restore a *status quo* insofar as possible, by placing the injured party in a position equivalent to that he had before the tort was committed.[10]

LIABILITY FOR TORTS

In the settlement of a dispute a nurse might be charged with unreasonable conduct that led to harm to another. The injured party must prove to the satisfaction of the court that the harm came about by the actions or inactions on the part of the accused. *Tort law* sets a standard for legal determination of fault, for fixing blame, and for measuring economic loss to the one injured.

One fixed and unconditional rule of law is that every person is liable for the torts that he commits. This axiom has often been overlooked or misunderstood by the community of professional nurses. For example, the physician's order has long been viewed as the sole legal responsibility of the physician and anyone sharing in its execution was not liable for any harm that followed, however erroneous the order may have been. It was also reasoned that since the physician was responsible, he could free the nurse from blame if the order were in error. However, the fact that other persons may have participated in, or even led, in action causing harm, never relieves one from tortious liability for his own acts to a third person. The physician, the employer of the nurse, and the nurse may all be joined in suit or held individually or collectively liable. *Potential liability for the nurse is never eliminated because of a particular relationship with others.*

The unprecedented rate of change in nursing has placed a consequent strain on the legal basis for its practice. In the foregoing chapters, it was demonstrated that revisions of statutory law reflect newly defined boundaries for nursing conduct. Statutory law, however, is but one source of legal

FIG. 4   Interdependence of statutory law and common law as a basis of authority for nursing practice.

authority governing nursing activities. Of equal importance, and highly relevant to all health professions, is that section of the common law known as tort law. A way to keep the distinction between these two areas of law is to recall that statutory law sets forth, in general terms, the functions that fall within the scope of nursing practice. In defining boundaries, it literally tells what the nurse *may do* or is legally permitted to do. When nursing conduct runs counter to this authorization for practice, either through failure to recognize its boundaries or failure to deliver the quality of care expected of a professional and harm comes to another because of this conduct, then court action against the nurse may follow. When the case is decided and the judicial decision is rendered, tort law is then written into the court record, stating what the nurse *did do* or was found innocent of doing and the financial responsibility, if any, for that conduct. Thus, the nurse melds both statutory law and common law to build a secure background for nursing practice (Fig. 4).

NEGLIGENCE OR MALPRACTICE

In the wide range of types of disputes that fall within the field of tort law, there is one area of particular importance to the health professional, namely, that in which a charge of negligence or malpractice is made against the one who is said to have brought about an injury. The terms "negligence" and "malpractice" are used interchangeably, although some authorities choose to distinguish between them by confining the use of the term "malpractice" to the negligent act or acts of a professional person.

In a popular sense, negligence is simply conduct that is lacking in due care. In a legal sense, *negligence or malpractice consists of the failure of a professional person to act in accordance with the prevalent professional standards or failure to foresee possibilities and consequences that a*

*professional person, having the necessary skill and training to act profes-
sionally, should foresee.*

Neither motive nor attitude enters into finding one culpable under negligence law. Nurses may be dedicated in the service rendered, but if their
actions go beyond the bounds of knowledge and the patient comes to
harm, nurses may be found to be at fault.

Clearly, there is a need to blend legal safety with health practice and
efficiency in quality care. The number of malpractice claims filed probably
does not represent the total picture of actual instances of harm that have
followed professional misconduct. Undoubtedly, many people do not seek
the courts to redress the harm suffered, for litigation is involved and
costly, and they may not perceive that their legal rights have been violated.
In many cases, a charge of malpractice is not supportable in court. Of
those claims that do come to trial, it should be recognized that in spite of
much publicity about malpractice cases and malpractice verdicts, it is estimated that a limited number are resolved in favor of the patient.

Today in all areas of living, people are more litigation-prone than in
former times, and they are more vocal in making known their rights, both
individually and collectively. It would seem that in the service-oriented
disciplines, such as nursing and medicine, there will always be suits and
threats of suits, for in their practice there is always the possibility of human errors of judgment in assessment and decision making.

A further complicating factor is that as medical science advances, practice becomes increasingly complex, risks are higher, and potential for
harm is ever greater. Although it is far from a gloomy picture, any attempt
to solve the problem solely by expanding insurance coverage is shortsighted in its negativism. A more positive approach is to take constructive
action to improve the quality of health care rather than seek a means of
circumventing legal action.

A primary concern for the health professional should be to find ways
of preventing litigation rather than to concern himself with procedures of
legal defense should harm occur. Constructive steps that are being taken
in this direction include peer review panels and increasing the authority of
regulatory agencies for disciplinary proceedings and supervision of professional practice. Continuing education for physicians and nurses to improve
the quality of care can go far in reducing the potential for litigation.

It is a fair assumption that a major reason for increasing malpractice
claims is the lowered and more impersonal quality of nursing and medical

care being given. What changes in the thinking and practice of the professional nurse could be made that would offer a blend of legal safety and better health care? Some answers are:

1. Know the relevant law and incorporate it into practice. Just as the physical, biologic, and social sciences have been made a part of every rational nursing decision, the law can be incorporated into practice as a safeguard for both the patient and the nurse.
2. Improve nurse-patient relationships; the satisfied patient seldom sues. At all times be aware of the rights of patients. Be alert to the importance of disclosure as a basis for consent.
3. Stay well within the area of individual competence. Undertake to perform only those tasks that one has the knowledge and skill to carry out.

PRECEDENT—A PRINCIPLE OF THE COMMON LAW

When a court decision is rendered, it becomes a part of the body of common law and as such serves a two-fold purpose. First, it settles a dispute and determines who won and who lost. If this were the end in itself, the common law would be an aggregate of isolated instances of controversies taken to court to resolve. The second purpose, however, is more far reaching in its consequences: the decision establishes a precedent for the resolution of future disputes in those situations in which the facts are similar.

Precendent may be governing in future litigation in one of two ways. It is binding when the decision has been made in a similar or higher court in the same state; it is persuasive when the decision is handed down by a court in another state. The principle of following precedent is known as the doctrine of "stare decisis," meaning "to stand as decided." This doctrine brings continuity, stability, and predictability to the law because the courts are not free to change legal rules with abandon.

While the law views precedent as important for the guidance of a dispute at hand, it need not be slavishly followed. Like statutory law, common law has a capacity for growth and change as social thinking fluctuates and new knowledge becomes available through scientific advancement. A statute that no longer reflects current nursing practice can be brought under legislative review for modification or repeal. Likewise, earlier judicial decisions can become outmoded and be subject to judicial review. The court can then, at its discretion, depart from precedent and write what has been termed "new law." A noted jurist, Roscoe Pound, once said, "law must be stable and yet it cannot stand still."[11]

Even a decision that has served as a precedent for many years may be changed. Any case is and should be open to scrutiny when advances in science point to the need for change. If fact, a balance should be maintained at all times between the need for stability and the need for change. Contrast the following two decisions: one that failed to move with advances in medical science and one in which new law was written because of the recognized need for change.

In the first instance a physician was held for negligence for incorrectly diagnosing pregnancy as a tumor and prescribing x-ray treatments in the later stages of pregnancy. Consequently, a child was born incapable of speech and action and without sight or hearing. In this case, the court chose to follow the long-standing rule that a child could not recover for injuries incurred prior to birth, even though at the time of the decision medical science had established that x-ray during pregnancy could cause damage to the central nervous system.[12]

In the second instance a pregnant woman was injured when she fell alighting from a bus. Her child was born prematurely, and subsequent heart trouble, jacksonian epilepsy, and inability to walk were claimed to result from the injuries in utero. The child sued the bus driver. The court, while recognizing the precedent that injury to an unborn child had previously been considered outside the scope of its protection, altered its views in light of medical advances and allowed recovery for any damages.[13]

PRECEDENT—A FORCE IN SHAPING NURSING CONDUCT

The interest of the professional nurse in the doctrine of precedent differs widely from that of the attorney. The attorney sees in the precedent of previous cases a significant basis for the argument that may be presented either for or against the client. In fact, the weight of the precedent of previous cases might determine the outcome of the dispute at hand. Cases for the attorney fall into a wide range of subjects, including personal injuries, corporate affairs, property claims, contracts, and many others. In each instance, a major part of the legal research is to seek the precedent that flows from relevant cases.

The professional nurse sees in the decision of a litigated case the precedent that is established in a particular area of conduct identified and considered by the law. Many questions arise for professional nurses in the examination of cases. When the court reviewed the conduct that brought about the harm, did it see it as conduct that fell within the range of nursing practice? Did it see the professional practitioner as capable of and responsible for independent practice? Did it see the professional nurse as qualified to make an assessment and arrive at a course of action? Did it see the nurse as a technician or a paramedical practitioner charged merely with the duty to follow the physician's orders?

The value of legal precedent as a tool for the improvement of nursing practice has been largely overlooked by the profession. When a judicial decision is looked upon as a means for examining current practice, it follows that it could be a force in improving the quality of care. For example, suppose a professional nurse erroneously selected the site for an injection and the patient came to harm. Suppose further that the instance was brought to the attention of the court, and that the judicial decision was that the nurse did not have, or, if she had, did not demonstrate, a sufficient knowledge of anatomy in selecting the site for the injection to avoid injury to the sciatic nerve. This decision would incorporate into law a precedent that recognized and required the use of scientific knowledge as a basis for nursing action.

In utilizing such a legal precedent, professional nurses might well study the facts of particular cases as a basis for curriculum changes. More important, perhaps, the precedent should cause nurses to examine seriously their knowledge of the scientific basis for actions now becoming current practice in expanding roles. The administration and supervision of parenteral fluids is one example of a therapy, often hazardous to the patient, that is now largely a nursing function. Fundamental principles governing fluid and electrolyte balance, circulatory dynamics, and drug interactions represent only a part of the knowledge essential to safe practice in this area.

If nurses have due regard for the importance of legal precedent, they will ask what the profession is doing to disseminate the substance of legal decisions to the nurse population and to evaluate its impact on current nursing practice. Also, it is important to analyze whether appropriate consideration is being given to the effect legal decisions may have on future professional goals.

DEPARTURE FROM PRECEDENT

When the court sees the need to depart from precedent, and has justi-
fication for doing so, its decision will introduce into the common law a
departure from a hitherto accepted principle. When this is done, the case
is cited as a "pathfinder," meaning that new law has been written that
will point the way for future legal consideration. For professional nursing,
a case that is a pathfinder may come in response to advances in nursing
science or a change in the public's expectation for the delivery of health
care. Illustrative of such a decision is the California case that found the
nurse derelict for failure to diagnose.[14] This was the first time that the
courts had viewed the act of diagnosis as a part of nursing practice. Partly
as a result of the precedent established in this case, the function of diagnosing has gradually been included in the statutory definition for practice
in many states.

Granted that professional nursing may long have been aware of the thin
line between the diagnosis by a physician and the diagnosis by a professional nurse, this decision nonetheless served to clarify the nurse's position. Identifying the nurse's role in diagnosing should not be looked upon
as a transfer of functions from the physician to the nurse. Rather, it recognizes that the diagnostic process is not the exclusive function of any one
health care profession.

Contrast the above decision regarding the nurse's role in diagnosis with
litigation in which the nurse was involved at the turn of the century. Note
the changing pattern of nursing responsibility in the court's interpretation
of the functions of the nurse. Early cases usually considered hospital or
physician responsible for the conduct of the nurse. Seldom was the nurse
ever held as a codefendant. Charges against nurses were generally for
functions of a custodial nature or for failure to seek the direction of the
physician.

A gradual shift to the precedent of today's litigation is reflected in the
decisions that view nurses as independent practitioners, being recognized
as such both in common law and in statutory law. Accountability for their
own acts is seen when they are sued as sole defendants or jointly as co-
defendants with the physician and/or the health care agency. Today's litigation in describing nursing conduct uses such terms as assessment, perceptive observation, and professional level of reporting. Colleague
relationships with the physician are discussed, rather than the subservient
role described in earlier cases. Illustrative of the changing judicial climate

are the two following cases, one which charges the nurse with giving substandard care and one which deals with the responsibility of the professional nurse for the quality of the total care of the patient.

Gugino v. Harvard Community Health Plan[15]

FACTS. Jeanne Gugino (plaintiff) seeks to recover damages for personal injuries as a result of alleged malpractice by defendants with respect to an intrauterine contraceptive device, the Dalkon Shield. The physician was also named as a codefendant, but the conduct of the professional nurse is the primary concern in evaluating the standard of conduct. The device was implanted in 1972. In 1974, the plaintiff consulted with the doctor concerning some dysfunctioning and bleeding. The doctor reassured her. From then on, her calls were answered by the registered nurse, also an employee of the Plan. The patient reported a foul vaginal order and was told to douche with yogurt. A week later when she reported pain, she was told it was probably gastrointestinal flu and that she should call back if she developed a fever. Later, on a scheduled appointment, the device was removed by the physician, and she was given an antibiotic and a drug for pain. On a return visit, multiple abscesses were diagnosed and the patient underwent a total hysterectomy.

CONDUCT OF NURSE. The court stated that the defendants, doctor and nurse, were under a continuing obligation to inform the plaintiff of the risks known to be associated with the Dalkon Shield (supported by articles from medical periodicals and newspapers). Failure to inform was negligence, and the omission of such disclosure probably determined the plaintiff's retention of the device and contributed to the infection. To quote from the case:

> The management of the plaintiffs' case by the defendant nurse, months later, was clearly in error; a yogurt douche is a substandard lay remedy, inappropriate for an odor of dead fish. Delay of more than forty-eight hours in scheduling diagnosis and treatment was substandard care. The time factor was critical and each day of delay increased the likelihood of surgery; this critical delay was the factor which caused the need for a total hysterectomy.

The impact of this precedent shows the need for professional nurses to operate from a knowledge basis that is being continually broadened, either through formal or informal study. Had the nurse been current in her knowledge, she would have been sensitive to the patient's warnings and would have given more timely advice.

Applebaum v. Board of Directors of Barton Memorial Hospital[16]

FACTS. The controversy began when the head nurse and night supervisor expressed concern to the hospital administrator about the quality of care being given to a patient by Dr. Applebaum. The hospital administrator transmitted the nurses' complaints to the Chief of the Medical Staff, who requested an investigation pursuant to the hospital's bylaws. As grounds for this request, the Chief of Staff listed incompetence in the performance of deliveries and care of the newborn, unauthorized use of experimental drugs, falsification of medical records, and improper conduct of labor. The investigation was carried on by the medical staff on a peer review basis.

Of interest to note in terms of the precedent established by this case is the case of *Darling versus Charleston Community Hospital,*[17] in which the nurses observed and made notes on the chart that reflected the quality of medical attention that was being given to a deteriorating patient, but on which they took no positive action. In the above and more recent case, the questionable quality of medical care was observed and positive action was taken through proper administrative channels.

NURSING ACCOUNTABILITY BASED ON THE COMMON LAW OF TORTS

The relevance of the common law of torts to nursing becomes apparent when one reflects on the nature of the profession. Nursing exists because people have health-related needs that they themselves cannot meet. It follows, then, that in the practice of their profession nurses must, either directly or indirectly, enter into a relationship that involves decision making with action that directly affects the life and well-being of another. Threaded through this action-oriented relationship are knowledge, judgment, and skills for which the nurse alone is accountable.

As has been explained, the common law of torts provides the means for those who claim harm to seek restitution through court action. The nurse who is knowledgeable concerning the scope and meaning of tort law adds one more dimension to the decision-making process. In so doing the element of risk is reduced and the quality of care is upgraded.

The hypothetical situations that follow illustrate relatively uncomplicated nursing activities that led to court action. In both instances such
action grew out of patient dissatisfaction with care directly traceable to
nursing conduct.

The court speaks to nurses about nursing

FACTS. Sylvia Hunt has been employed in the clinic of a small manufacturing company for 2 years. She is directly responsible to the company
physician who has clinic hours three afternoons a week. Sylvia enjoys her
work, which primarily involves health teaching and caring for minor illnesses and injuries. In carrying out the latter, she relies on standing orders
and protocols that have been set down by the company physician.

Early in January, Mike Jones reported to the clinic complaining of
general malaise, sore throat, hoarseness, and cough. After a review of
symptoms, a throat culture, and physical assessment, Sylvia recommended
the clinic's routine treatment for upper respiratory infections. Three weeks
later Mr. Jones returned, symptom-free except for persistent hoarseness.
After reviewing his health history, Sylvia recommended throat lozenges
and advised him to cut down on smoking. Two more visits followed, during which Sylvia and Mr. Jones explored the problem and made plans to
limit certain activities that might be causing laryngeal irritation. After both
visits, Sylvia recorded on Mr. Jones' record that he believed the hoarseness was lessening.

In April, Mike Jones consulted a private physician who, after laryngeal
examination, advised hospitalization for surgery. A partial laryngectomy
was performed for removal of a benign tumor. Mr. Jones recovered but
with voice changes that he believed could have been avoided by earlier
diagnosis. Convinced of this, he brought suit against the clinic and the
clinic nurse, Sylvia Hunt.

ANALYSIS. Sylvia's experience of being sued, although traumatic for
her, offers her professional colleagues a valuable lesson in the need for
thorough reassessment when a health problem persists. It is not the purpose of this analysis to determine whether Sylvia was found negligent in
caring for Mike Jones or whether his assumption that an earlier diagnosis
would have ensured a more favorable response was correct. That is a task
for the courts. What is important is to consider criteria by which Sylvia's
conduct might be judged and to question why such conduct occurred.

It is no longer possible to justify Sylvia's conduct on the basis that
"nurses are not allowed to diagnose." Professional nurses have long rec-

ognized that identifying a patient's problem is an integral part of the nursing process. Today, many nurse practice acts recognize that diagnosing is a function of professional nursing practice.

In any event, to defend the nurse's action in this instance by focusing on the act of diagnosis would ignore the conduct that led up to the court action and would deny the fact that nurses are legally accountable for their actions. To have seen and evaluated a patient's status over a period of 3 months without taking more positive action than is indicated in this situation strongly suggests negligence. Apparently, Sylvia relied entirely on the patient's subjective appraisal of his symptoms. Since it is common knowledge that persistent hoarseness is one of the danger signs of cancer, surely it is to be expected that a professional nurse would be held accountable for such knowledge and that her failure to take steps to rule out a laryngeal tumor would be seriously questioned.

In responding to a similar fact pattern, *Cooper versus National Motor Bearing Co.*, in which the nurse was held accountable, the court reasoned that:

> A patient is entitled to an ordinary careful physical examination, such as the circumstances, the condition of the patient, and the nurse's opportunity for examination will permit. If there is reasonable opportunity for examination, and the nature of the injury or ailment can be discovered by the exercise of ordinary care and treatment, then the nurse is answerable for failure to make such a discovery.[18]

The precedent established in the above decision should assist nurses in determining whether Sylvia exercised "ordinary care" in the management of Mr. Jones' problem. If not, did her actions suggest a reluctance to follow accepted standards of professional nursing practice and to confront the problem in a decisive manner? Furthermore, they might explore the circumstances that exist within educational programs and work situations which might cause any professional nurse to fail to assume an assertive role in the exercise of professional practice. To examine conduct only to determine fault will contribute little to improve practice. To search for the causes of failure is one means by which nursing will make a significant contribution to future health care.

A tale of two patients

FACTS. Jean Collins, R.N., is a team leader on an active surgical service at Fairhaven Hospital. On the morning of June 6 she had twelve patients under her care, four of whom were scheduled for surgery. Assisting her were two practical nurses and an orderly.

One of the peroperative patients, Mr. Isaacs, age 72, was scheduled for a hernia repair and was assigned to the orderly for routine morning care. Before administering his preoperative medication, Nurse Collins discussed with Mr. Isaacs and his wife the surgical procedure and what he might expect in the immediate postoperative period. She also cautioned him that after the preoperative medication was administered he must remain in bed and explained why.

An hour later, disregarding both the nurse's warning and his wife's protests, Mr. Isaacs got up to go to the bathroom. Unsteady on his feet, he fell and fractured his right wrist. In the meantime, Nurse Collins had recorded on Mr. Isaacs' chart the medication administered, her instruction, and the patient's response.

■   ■   ■

Across the city in Fairmont Hospital, Joan Andrews, R.N., began her day as a team leader with a staff of two practical nurses and a nurse's aide. She, too, had twelve patients with three scheduled for surgery. Among these was Mr. Johnson, age 73, scheduled for a hernia repair at 9:00 A.M.

At 8:00 A.M., Nurse Andrews, who had assigned one of the practical nurses to give routine care to Mr. Johnson, brought in his preoperative medication. After asking Mrs. Johnson to leave the room, she asked the patient if he had had surgery before. He stated that he had and that he knew "all about it." She administered the drug, readmitted Mrs. Johnson and left to chart the medication on the patient's record. One hour later Mr. Johnson got out of bed, unassisted, and en route to the bathroom fell and fractured his left wrist.

ANALYSIS. In the preceding incidents many similarities and some significant differences are apparent. In both situations we have a professional nurse team leader with a like case load and nursing staff engaged in the preoperative preparation of two patients, alike in age and diagnosis.

What is significantly different is that Nurse Collins did not make ill-founded assumptions regarding her patient's knowledge of the situation, whereas Nurse Andrews accepted Mr. Johnson's statement that he knew what it was "all about" without even determining the nature or date of his prior surgery. Nurse Collins also included Mrs. Isaacs in the preoperative teaching, and in so doing cemented the patient-nurse-family relationship and added one more person to the nursing team, Mrs. Isaacs. Nurse Andrews excluded Mrs. Johnson and thus failed not only to foster goodwill but left the room, leaving behind two persons ignorant of the potential for harm in a situation in which they were the key people. Nurse Collins carefully recorded on Mr. Isaacs' chart the teaching she had done and her evaluation of the patient's response. Nurse Andrews made no reference on the patient's chart of her brief interchange with Mr. Johnson.

The Isaacs accepted the accident as an unfortunate complication that could have been avoided if Mr. Isaacs had followed either the nurse's direction or his wife's warning. The Johnsons brought suit against the hospital and Nurse Andrews, claiming negligence. There appears to be considerable evidence to sustain that charge. Had you been asked, as an expert witness, to evaluate Joan Andrews' nursing care, what would have been your response?

Summary

In the preceding hypothetical situations it is safe to assume that both nurses charged with negligence lacked a full understanding of their legal duty to their patient. Had either of them been conversant with the common law of torts, how it evolves and how it protects the public from harm, it is quite likely that the alleged negligence would not have occurred. The nursing process unfolds as multiple factors are fitted together to produce a plan of care. It can be argued that the greater the amount of relevant data, concepts, and ideas synthesized in that process, the more appropriate will be the action that follows.

The common law of torts is both fixed and fluid. Its unique flexibility and ability to move with change enables it to decide disputes arising from situations that never before occurred. This characteristic will be carried into Section Two, which will examine conduct legally relevant to the role of the professional nurse.

Section two

THE REASONABLY PRUDENT NURSE

In Section One, statutory and common law were examined as the sources of legal authority governing nursing practice. Secure in her knowledge of the law, Patricia Guise began to deal with a situation, described in the Introduction to this text, in which she identified the need for a change in the medical regimen. Like many of her colleagues, Patricia is a knowledgeable risk taker, confident in her ability to make nursing decisions in the best interests of her patients. Any reluctance to question the adequacy of the physician's orders was overcome by her understanding of the legal meaning of an acceptable standard of care and the duty of affirmative action.

In the initial step of the nursing process—assessment—Patricia was confronted with a deteriorating patient and a medical regimen that offered little support. Acting with reason and prudence, she acknowledged legal boundaries within which nursing judgments are made and the decision-making process is set in motion. Furthermore, her knowledge of the law reinforced Patricia's awareness that any evaluation of her conduct would be based on an estimate of the degree to which she had subscribed to an accepted standard of care. Implicit in such a standard would be the understanding that the appraisal of a patient's condition must project beyond what the nurse observed to any change that might follow. In short, a nursing practitioner is charged, by the profession and the public, with the responsibility to foresee harm and the duty to act in such a manner as to minimize the probability of that harm occurring.

Although Patricia understood the chain of command and flow of authority governing the administrative policy of Memorial Hospital, she saw herself not only as an employee but also as a professional working in an interdependent relationship with her peers. She recognized that if her second effort to communicate her concerns regarding Mrs. Yancey failed, she would be forced to act counter to generally accepted policy. Failure to act affirmatively at this point would be setting institutional procedure and interprofessional relationships above the patient's right to care. This she could not do, either ethically or legally.

By integrating a knowledge of substantive law into assessment and decision making, Patricia could act more aggressively and confidently in carrying out her duty to Mrs. Yancey. The ensuing chapters will examine in greater detail the legal concept of the reasonably prudent nurse. Such content illustrates how knowledge of the law reduces the level of anxiety, which is a natural component of decision making, and helps to ensure quality care and improved nursing practice. Finally, the imposition of liability for care that fails to measure up to an acceptable standard and the use of the professional nurse as expert witness in the evaluation of the quality of nursing care will be discussed.

4

Standard of care

One of the attributes of any society is the repeated and predictable occurrence of accidental injury. The causes of such injuries are many, with the automobile leading by a wide margin. These accidents often cause serious physical, emotional, and financial injury. The victim who is physically or emotionally harmed may have no recourse but to suffer the consequence of the injury. If, however, the harm also results in financial loss, the individual does have a recourse under certain defined circumstances, and that recourse is to the law. Tort law is in significant measure a field of law designed to allocate the financial losses from various kinds of accidental injuries.

Nurse practitioners as average citizens are, from a legal perspective, not overly concerned with the allocation of loss from automobile accidents or airplane crashes. Although they may be involved in any one of various kinds of accidents, their professional relationships with the world at large are not affected and whether one is a nurse or any other professional is irrelevant in assessing responsibility for an injury such as one caused by making a U turn illegally.

Nurses are vitally interested from a professional point of view, however, in the legal handling of losses owing to accidents occurring within their professional sphere, that is, how they can be allocated, on what basis, why, and to whom. Allocation, as used here, simply means the payment of money. A legal decision does not attempt to ''allocate'' emotional injury or broken legs. It attempts to allocate the financial side, namely, money, and by allocation or reallocation takes money from one person and gives it to another, who has been injured.

When and under what conditions will nurses have to respond with money to compensate a patient who has been injured by their conduct or whose condition or injuries have been aggravated by their conduct? Against what standard will conduct be measured? The answer comes from a part of the body of common law that has created a standard known as the "conduct of the reasonably prudent man." As numerous decisions have been made over the years, the courts have created a fictitious image of the reasonably prudent man. His conduct is that against which the conduct of others will be measured. No one has ever seen the reasonable man; he is not a superman; he is average in intelligence, judgment, foresight, and skill. "It is sometimes said that the study of negligence is the study of the mistakes that a reasonable man might make."[1]

THE REASONABLY PRUDENT NURSE

How can this standard be applied to nursing? The professional nurse must perform at a level that equals or exceeds that of a reasonably prudent practitioner, utilizing the knowledge and skills of the profession. If in any circumstance or situation nurses fail to meet this standard, and in the event that their conduct, falling below the standard, causes injury to another, they may be required to compensate the other party for injuries so caused.

Thus stated in general terms, the principle seems clear, but its application may be the subject of considerable controversy. What, for example, is the conduct of a "reasonably prudent nurse"? What are the "necessary knowledge" and "necessary skills"? There may be significant disagreement about these matters in many instances, but the basic guiding principle of the reasonably prudent nurse nonetheless remains.

It is essential to keep in mind that this legal standard is not applied in the abstract, nor is it applied to punish, discipline, or chastise. As mentioned earlier nurses may be guilty of the most flagrant unprofessional conduct in the course of practice, and yet not experience legal liability because, in spite of their shortcomings, the gods smile on them—and on their patients—and no injury occurs. If no injury occurs, there is no loss; if there is no loss, there is no occasion for allocation of any loss. Therefore the "reasonable man" standard will not be invoked, although the nurse may, as we have seen in an earlier chapter, be subject to disciplinary proceedings for various kinds of unprofessional conduct.

AMERICAN NURSES' ASSOCIATION STANDARDS
FOR PROFESSIONAL NURSING PRACTICE

The professional nurse, or others who seek to evaluate nursing conduct, can look to the American Nurses' Association to determine what the profession holds to be acceptable standards of practice. Working through its membership, the Association has developed standards for various specialty areas, as well as generic standards applicable to all nurses in all areas of practice. These standards and the accompanying assessment factors, which can be used to determine if the standards have been met, provide a framework for judging whether a particular nursing action fell within the realm of acceptable practice. For example, a standard which states that

Nursing diagnoses are derived from health status data[2]

is a criterion by which the quality of nursing could be judged. The degree to which this standard has been met becomes important when one analyzes questionable nursing conduct in terms of the assessment factors associated with this particular standard:

1. The client's/patient's health status is compared to the norm in order to determine if there is deviation from the norm and the degree and direction of deviation.
2. The client's/patient's capabilities and limitations are identified.
3. The nursing diagnoses are related to and congruent with the diagnoses of all other professionals caring for the client/patient.[2]

Since these standards represent the opinions of nurses engaged in professional practice, and since they have been promulgated by the professional association, nurses would be well served by consistently referring to them in evaluating whether their own conduct or the conduct of others is that of a reasonably prudent nurse.

STANDARD OF CARE FOR THE EXPANDING NURSING ROLE

The standard of conduct of the reasonable man is a flexible one, which has proved over the years that it can accommodate itself to the pace of rapid social change. This legal principle is important to fields that are shifting as rapidly as are nursing and medicine. For example, contrast the knowledge and skill expected of the nurse who was found negligent for placement of hot water bottles near a semiconscious patient to that expected of the nurse responsible for monitoring fetal heart tones who failed to take action when the condition of the unborn child became alarming.

To keep pace with change, the nursing profession is emphasizing the need for nurses to continually update knowledge and skills as roles in the delivery of health care shift and as new knowledge becomes available. Today some states not only license, but also certify some nurses to function in particular areas of specialization. Those who deal with advances in knowledge must keep abreast of it. What might be understandable ignorance today may be negligence tomorrow.

The following description of the expanded role provides for flexibility in the event the standard of nursing care comes under legal review:

> The nurse who practices in an expanded role performs increasingly complex acts in health and medical care and possesses a scientific background which permits legally defensible decisions in clinical judgments as advances in physical, biological and social sciences, relevant to the service being rendered, become available.

Since the preceding statement deals in generalities, there may be differences of opinion in regard to its application to practice. How does the conduct of ''a reasonably prudent nurse'' acting in an expanded role differ from that of any other nurse practitioner? What are the ''necessary knowledge'' and ''necessary skills'' required to perform complex acts? The basic guiding principle of the reasonably prudent man holds. The nurse who offers services to the public by virtue of having certain specialized knowledge and skill would be measured against the standard of conduct of the community of professionals in that specialty.

RISK TAKING—A FACTOR IN HEALTH CARE

In every health care situation there are two categories of risk takers— the recipient of health care and the health care giver. As nursing and medical science advance and become more complex, risk mounts for both the patient and the practitioner. Knowledgeable practitioners, therefore, school themselves to recognize the potential for risk to the patient and realize that the manner in which they deal with risk is one measure of conduct.

Of first importance is the risk to the patient or health care recipient. In considering what constitutes an acceptable standard of care for the reasonably prudent nurse, one must take into account the extent to which the patient was protected from unreasonable risk of harm. In all of nursing, but particularly in high-risk areas, the wise practitioner proceeds with caution, continually assessing and analyzing the patient's response to treatment. Thus, the professional nurse responsible for a patient with septic shock must be aware that the etiologic factors of this condition are different and less well understood than those of hypovolemic shock, and will use this knowledge to provide the kind of professional surveillance that will detect signs of a worsening shock state.

The law could not and does not require that professional actions be risk free. There are always calculated risks. Calculated risks can be categorized into two areas. First, there is the statistical risk in which an unfavorable result can be forecast in a given number of cases. Such a risk can be programmed on a computer and converted into a mathematical probability. The nurse who is aware of the statistical risk associated with a specific treatment regimen has the advantage of being able to project into the nursing care plan actions designed to reduce the known risk to the patient. For example, if the nurse knows that a certain percentage of patients undergoing gastric surgery develop dumping syndrome, the plan of care can be directed toward both detecting early symptoms and carrying out nursing actions that might prevent their occurrence.

The second type of calculated risk is one involving judgment. If, for example, the condition of a patient is critical and the risk of administering a central nervous system depressant is high, the benefits to the patient must outweigh the risk to be taken. Moreover, in order to minimize risk, the nurse is obliged to exercise extreme care in observing the patient's response to the drug. A calculated risk is never a defense for negligent conduct or for deviation from an acceptable standard of practice.

In health care a risk can be assumed by the person who is in the position to obtain the possible benefits from the suggested therapy. Patients may refuse a treatment, or, when they have been made aware of the consequences of the decision, they may choose to assume the risk and waive liability for any harm that might result. Legally, in such a waiver the patient never assumes the risk for a lowered standard of care. Nurses, like physicians, hold a position because of education and experience, and their conduct will be reviewed against that background in any charge of harm flowing from the mismanagement of a high-risk situation.

THE PROFESSIONAL NURSE—A KNOWLEDGEABLE RISK TAKER

Nurses may subject patients to unreasonable risk if the former lack knowledge or fail to use knowledge to recognize the inherent danger of the situation. In either instance the conduct might be viewed as reckless or irresponsible, for it would fail to meet the standard of care of a reasonably prudent practitioner of professional nursing. Often the risk to the patient becomes clear only after harm has occurred. When this happens, it is doubtful that the nurse assessed the situation adequately before making a judgment to act or withhold action. Reasonably prudent conduct must be perceived in advance, and then, if a risk is to be taken, it is with full knowledge of the potential consequences. The professional nurse should not shun risk; it should be viewed positively with an awareness that the ability to deal adequately with risk is commensurate with the knowledge one brings to the situation.

Risk taking by the nurse has certain guidelines that should be so well understood they can be applied in a crisis, where assessment must be followed immediately by action, as well as in more relaxed situations that allow time for deliberation. The law sets boundaries that, in a sense, both limit and extend risk taking by the nurse. For instance, in the definition for nursing practice in the hypothetical State of X, authority is granted for a number of functions that deal with diagnosing and treating human responses to actual or potential health problems. The definition does, however, limit risk taking in nursing conduct by prescribing that the nursing regimen shall be consistent with and shall not vary the medical regimen. In defining what the nurse may and may not do, the law sets limits on risk taking, yet the principle of standard of care sets the measure of how well the function must be carried out and therein lies the challenge, and possibly the risk, for the nurse.

There are guidelines for risk taking to be found in the common law of torts. For example, the nurse who, in compliance with hospital policy, left a heavily sedated patient so that she could accompany a doctor on his rounds was found negligent when the sedated patient fell from the bed and was injured.[3] Decisions such as this set precedents for nursing conduct by ruling that the nurse violated a standard of care through failure to take action that ran counter to hospital policy. The nurse failed to assess the inherent risk to the patient and thus needlessly proceeded to act in a manner that placed her professional career at risk.

There are limitations on risk taking by the nurse set by health care agencies through standing orders and protocols and by the interdisciplinary rules and regulations of boards of nursing and boards of medical examiners. For instance, to qualify for the staff of a newborn air transport service, the agency may require the nurse to have definite preparation and experience to deal with the potential problems of asphyxia, shock, and cardiac arrest in an unusual environment. These kinds of regulatory procedures minimize risks for nurses by barring them from positions requiring knowledge and skills they do not have. More important, it ensures the patient, although in critical condition, the security of having care given by a nurse who is a knowledgeable risk taker in a specialized area of practice.

THE NURSING PROCESS RELIES ON STANDARDS OF CARE

Unlike computers, nurses are not programmed to respond in a set way to a given set of circumstances. Every significant nursing action must be deliberated and weighed in terms of the probable outcome. This deliberation either delineates the single most appropriate action or points out alternative courses of action from which the nurse is free to choose the direction to be taken. Throughout this process the nurse must be guided by a standard of care that provides a baseline for the assessment, decision making, and action that ultimately translate into safe, effective nursing practice.

In the hypothetical situations that follow, claims of negligence were voiced by a patient and by a relative of a patient. In one instance the patient came to harm and court action followed, while in the other, harm did not result and the claim was not pursued. As you study the situations, determine whether or not you believe either nurse had, at any point, knowingly weighed his or her judgment or conduct against an accepted standard of care.

Reasonable judgment or unreasonable risk?

FACTS. Officer Burns was admitted to the surgical intensive care unit of Northwood General Hospital following emergency surgery. He had suffered a gunshot wound, and his condition was regarded as serious. During the operative procedure, an intracatheter was introduced into a hand vein and an infusion of glucose in saline solution to which levarterenol (Levophed) had been added was started.

Gary Owens, R.N., was in charge of the nursing team responsible for

Officer Burns' care. Before the surgeon left the intensive care unit, he reviewed his postoperative orders with Gary, placing much emphasis on the difficulty encountered in introducing the catheter into the vein and the great need for continuing the levarterenol drip until the blood pressure stabilized.

Two hours later Officer Burns' hand showed distinct swelling at the infusion site. Gary lowered the intravenous bottle and noted a good blood return in the intracatheter. On the basis of this observation he decided that the intravenous infusion was functioning adequately, and that it was in the best interest of the patient not to discontinue the treatment or to attempt another venipuncture. However, infiltration of the tissues was occurring. Severe sloughing of the tissues of the involved hand followed, resulting in prolonged treatment requiring plastic surgery and physical therapy. Officer Burns sued Northwood General Hospital and Gary Owens for negligence, which allegedly led to the loss of the use of his hand for 1 year.

ANALYSIS. To determine whether Gary Owens was negligent in caring for Officer Burns, it is necessary to consider only one act or failure to act—the decision to allow the levarterenol infusion to continue. Is this a judgment one would expect of a reasonably prudent nurse?

Swelling of the tissues of the hand had been observed, and it is reasonable to assume it was caused by infiltration of the intravenous solution. Although lowering of the intravenous bottle had produced a flow of blood through the catheter, it is also reasonable to expect a nurse in Gary Owens' position to be aware that extravasation of fluid at the point where the needle had entered the vein could occur or that repeated attempts to enter the vein could have resulted in several penetrations of the vein wall, which would permit leakage of fluid into the tissues.

Since it has been well established that levarterenol is a powerful vaso-constrictor, it could be expected that a professional nurse would realize that infiltration of an intravenous solution containing levarterenol could cause local vasoconstriction and tissue necrosis.

Gary Owens testified that he was aware of the properties of levarterenol, but he had determined that the need for circulatory support outweighed the danger of tissue slough from infiltration.

The decision as to Gary's guilt or innocence rests with the court, but professional nurses reviewing the facts of the case might well ask themselves (1) whether Gary's conduct in this instance was that of a reasonably prudent nurse; (2) whether he gave sufficient consideration to alternative courses of action in reaching his decision; and (3) whether his argument that the patient's need for circulatory support outweighed the danger of local tissue damage subjected the patient to unreasonable risk.

Practice based on principle—reasonable nursing conduct?

FACTS. Molly Ferguson was a capable nurse. For the past 4 years she had been employed at Beth El Hospital as evening charge nurse on Second South. Molly was active professionally, often participating in educational programs and workshops to improve nursing practice.

Virginia Essex had been hospitalized at Beth El for 6 weeks before she was transferred to Molly's unit. Complications following bowel surgery had left her in a generally debilitated condition. Because of Virginia's inability to tolerate solid food, her physician elected to initiate intravenous hyperalimentation, a procedure new to Beth El and to the city. Treatment was begun shortly after Mrs. Essex was transferred to Second South.

Molly's introduction to the patient and the procedure came when she reported on duty at 3:00 P.M. At the change of shift report, the head nurse explained that the hyperalimentation infusate, a concentrated glucose and protein solution, had been started at 9:00 A.M. and was to be delivered into the patient's left subclavian vein at a constant flow rate. The nursing supervisor added that she was in the process of securing information about the procedure and would have it on the unit at soon as possible.

Uneasy because of her limited knowledge of the patient and the treatment, Molly observed Mrs. Essex closely. Concern for her patient mounted as she observed a gradual increase in pulse rate and an excessive urinary output. At 6:00 P.M., a dramatic change occurred—a marked fall in blood pressure accompanied by a rapid pulse and deepening lethargy. Her physician was called and shortly thereafter was at the bedside. He attributed the symptoms to osmotic dehydration caused by too rapid infusion of glucose and reprimanded Molly for not checking urinary sugars and modifying the intravenous flow rate.

Mr. Essex arrived for a visit with his wife and, alarmed by the obvious change in her condition, demanded an explanation. The physician reviewed what had happened and what was being done to rectify the situation. Frustrated and angry, Mr. Essex threatened to sue the hospital, the physician, and Molly Ferguson.

ANALYSIS. Eventually Mrs. Essex recovered, and Mr. Essex's threat did not materialize. The event, however, was not forgotten by Molly Ferguson. Believing that the matter had not been sufficiently explored, she initiated a group discussion of the incident.

The discussion focused principally on whether Molly had been negligent in her care of Mrs. Essex. It was asked: could a nurse be held to a standard of care that was based on knowledge not available at the time the alleged negligence occurred? Molly and her colleagues on the nursing staff argued that she could not have been expected to act in such a way as to forestall dehydration since she had no prior knowledge of possible complications and could not have had since hyperalimentation had not, at the time, been reported in the nursing literature or explored in any continuing education program in the area. They also raised the question as to whether the physician or nursing supervisor had a duty to exercise greater care in clarifying the potential dangers in a treatment unfamiliar to the professional nursing staff.

Others, among them the physician and the nursing supervisor, maintained that Molly or any other professional person had the obligation to question if they did not fully understand a treatment regimen. Furthermore, in this instance, she should have recognized that the symptoms forewarned impending physiologic imbalance. This recognition would have led her to relate the symptoms to the nature of the intravenous solution and caused her to suspect glucose overloading. In short, they held that nursing should be based on knowledge, not on procedure, and that failure to utilize known scientific principles in determining nursing action did not measure up to an acceptable standard of professional care.

Rather than continue to focus on Molly's conduct, the hospital's legal representative suggested that the incident reflected a breakdown in communications and proposed that, in the future, a physician initiating a new treatment regimen should be asked to fully acquaint the nursing staff with its purpose and inherent dangers. This recommendation was endorsed by the physician as well as the nursing staff.

Molly Ferguson's care of Mrs. Essex may not have been exemplary, but her decision to explore her conduct in open discussion was. Although a consensus regarding a standard of care was not reached, it can be assumed that each participant was made more aware of his legal accountability for patient care and more concerned with the need for sharing information among those responsible for that care. By taking a positive approach to the threat of court action and not allowing it to impede an honest appraisal of what happened, the group came to a greater appreciation of the law as an instrument for upgrading patient care and professional practice.

Summary

In the preceding situations, both Gary Owens and Molly Ferguson found themselves in the awkward position of having been labeled incompetent. Both were serious practitioners, both held responsible positions, and yet both were compelled, one by court action and one by threat of court action, to defend their actions before others. In all probability, their problems could have been avoided if they had schooled themselves to think and act in terms of what an acceptable standard of care would be in a given set of circumstances. Since professional nursing has its roots in critical assessment based on knowledge of physical, biologic, and social sciences, the effort of weighing a judgment or action against a standard of reasonableness should not be too burdensome.

5

Legal duty

America is said to be a nation of spectators and a nation of spectator-critics. It is easy to sit back and watch someone else attempt to carry out a difficult task and then to criticize the results. Moreover, the lack of responsibility for bringing about those results makes it a harmless game in which there are no losers among the spectators.

Professional nursing does not fall into a category that permits one to sit back and watch another win or lose. Once a nurse-patient relationship comes into being, the law automatically imposes a legal duty on the nurse for the welfare of the patient. This responsibility far exceeds those normally owed by the general public to one another, although all members of society are required to conduct themselves in such a way that harm to others will be avoided.

A charge of negligence cannot be established against a nurse unless there has been a failure to measure up to a proper standard of care or failure to discharge a legal duty when one is owed. As the health care system becomes more complex, the legal duty of the nurse is extended. Because nursing is an essential link in the chain of health care, the nurse has a duty to act in the event of a breakdown in patient care, wherever in the chain that breakdown occurs. This means the nurse is never permitted, under the law, passively to observe inferior care. The most common situation is of a physician or fellow nurse demonstrably or clearly failing to provide the appropriate care to patients, but it also may come about because a hospital or other health care agency is failing to exercise its corporate duty of providing quality care. Under both of these circumstances, the nurse must act and cannot hide behind the fact that "the doctor knows best" or "the administration doesn't listen to nurses."

Like the word "law," duty has many meanings. It can be described as a relationship that derives from a sense of moral or ethical obligation to one's fellowmen. In a legal sense, however, duty refers to an obligation to behave toward others in certain ways as defined by the courts.

The duty to carry out properly and appropriately the tasks one undertakes is a familiar one. The nurse clearly recognizes that once a task is undertaken it must be done competently and thoroughly. The duty to inject one's self into the stream of patient care wherever a problem arises is perhaps less familiar but equally compelling. For example, a nurse responsible for the care of a patient or a group of patients has a duty to intervene if the quality of care given by the other health personnel falls short of meeting the patient's needs.

To extend the scope of duty further, a nurse not directly responsible for the care of the patient but aware that the quality of care has broken down, has a duty either to act alone or to refer the problem to one who has the authority to intervene.

For nurses, ethical, moral, and legal duties so meld that it is difficult to distinguish which is the controlling force. The law is clear in leaving ethical and moral duties to the conscience of the offender, but if a legal duty is breached and injury follows, liability is imposed.

DUTY OF AFFIRMATIVE ACTION

The duty to take affirmative action is but a part of the larger legal duty of the nurse, which is to conduct one's professional practice in such a way as to achieve positive results and to avoid, insofar as possible, harm that is foreseeable. Inaction can just as readily lead to injury as can misguided, inappropriate, or incompetent action. It is because nurses place themselves, willingly and knowingly, in situations where their conduct, be it active or passive, can lead to injury that this legal duty is of such importance in nursing.

Unless a special relationship exists, a person does not have a legal duty to save another from harm, provided that he is not the one bringing about the harm. But failure to act is not a shield against liability if a duty is owed; failure to act is itself a decision just as significant as a decision to act. Generally, the roadside automobile accident or the drowning person imposes no legal responsibility on anyone to intervene. Should one decide to do so, however, he would be required to exercise a reasonable standard of care and judgment. Nurses or physicians who intervene in emergencies are held to the duty to conduct themselves in accordance with professional, and not lay, standards.

Professional nurses have been held to be negligent when they failed to observe a duty to take affirmative action when confronted with a steadily deteriorating condition in a patient and medical care that was either not available or not of the quality necessary to deal with the problem. Under these circumstances, the courts have ruled that it is the duty of the nurse to take positive and even forceful steps to bring the situation under control. In the case of *Goff v. Doctors General Hospital,*[4] the patient died of hemorrhage following childbirth when an incision of the cervix had been made by the physician to relieve a constrictive band of muscle. In holding for the husband of the deceased, the court stated: The nurses knew of the peril of the mother, knew the cause and origin of the peril, and their inaction was sufficient to show negligent conduct in professional practice, even though in his own right, the physician was also negligent in numerous respects. To act or to decide not to act is a positive decision that falls within the exercise of one's duty of affirmative action. In nursing practice there are often conflicts in deciding to whom a first duty is owed: the employer, the physician, or the patient. Ideally, the goals of the first two would never be in conflict with the welfare of the third. However, at times the nurse has a legal duty to act independently in the interest of the patient, even though such actions run counter to hospital policy or the physician's orders.

DUTY TO FORESEE HARM AND TO ELIMINATE RISKS

The level of legal accountability of the health care practitioner to the patient is directly related to the standard of care required in a given situation. The greater the risk of harm to the patient the greater the legal duty of the professional to act in such a way as to minimize or eliminate the risk. Legally significant examples of failure to foresee harm and to eliminate risks are illustrated by the surgical nurse who left the operating room without delegating responsibility for the sponge count and the nurse who failed to question an order for an anticoagulant even though the strength of the solution had been changed from 1:10,000 to 1:1,000.

The duty to foresee harm and eliminate risk lies at the very core of professional nursing practice and is both exciting and awesome. It is a sophisticated form of assessment that requires the use of knowledge and skill to forestall harm rather than simply dealing with events as they occur. Should harm occur, the court would question whether the risk could have been recognized by a reasonably prudent practitioner or whether it required perceptive ability beyond the scope of nursing practice. If the breach of duty was the result of a lack of understanding on the part of the nurse, one factor in measuring accountability would be when and how the nurse had updated his or her knowledge of recent advances in nursing and medical science. Certification in areas of specialization, participation in continuing education programs, advanced nursing courses, and a record of successful practice might be offered to show the nurse had acted responsibly in this respect.

COLLEAGUE RELATIONSHIPS

As nursing becomes more widely identified as a professional discipline, the nurse's role in relation to colleagues on the health team becomes more significant. The structure of the health care system today demands that health professionals not only use their individual knowledge and skills to attain their specific goals, but that they also work closely with each other to achieve shared team goals.

Since the functions of medicine and nursing often overlap, it is particularly important for professional nurses to recognize that both the physician and nurse have an obligation to develop relationships that allow for an interchange of ideas and opinions, and to implement a regimen in which professional goals are commensurate with the interests of the client/patient.

Professional nurses who find themselves in conflict with the physician, or any other member of the health team, have an obligation to discuss the matter with the professional with whom they disagree. If, as previously explained, any member of the team is thoroughly convinced that harm may come to a patient because of the conduct of a colleague, that member has the legal duty to attempt to prevent that harm from occurring. However, the duty to foresee harm and to take action to prevent that harm does not imply that a professional has the right to supplant the decision of another health team member merely because of a disagreement with the approach used. The health care recipient has the right to the services of a team that communicates with each other and that coordinates individual talents in developing the most effective health care plan possible.

While professional nursing must guard against any movement that could again place them in a subordinate position, this concern cannot be so overriding that it supersedes the needs of the person being cared for. It is important for nurses to acknowledge that, while their role is autonomous, it is also one of collaboration, on an equal footing, with other health team professionals. "Defining autonomy to mean 'not dependent' is perhaps more realistic and precise than defining it to mean 'independent.' This definition allows for what is actually sought in the role, namely, the interdependence of equal practitioners."[5]

FORESEEABILITY—THE CHALLENGE TO PROFESSIONAL NURSING

The nursing world is made up of persons of different educational backgrounds who often perform the same functions but with differing degrees of knowledge, skill, and accountability. The difficulty in distinguishing between professional and nonprofessional practice continues to frustrate nurse educators, health care administrators, and those whose task is to define nursing practice legally.

Perhaps the difference defies definition, but if one examines the concept of legal duty, particularly the duty to foresee harm, the differences become more apparent. True, the nonprofessional nurse is prepared to respond to clues of impending harm to a patient, but accountability can only be commensurate with the level of educational preparation. Consequently, the nonprofessional would be held to skills and nursing decisions that flow more or less from standardized or expected relationships, whereas professional conduct is more closely tied to judgment. The professional nurse is expected to synthesize scientific knowledge and observable data to arrive at a decision to act or withhold action. Mastery of technique is expected of all nurses, but the professional is expected, to a greater degree than the nonprofessional, to react responsibly to the unusual or unpredictable in the execution of a particular technique.

In the hypothetical situations that follow, examine the conduct of the professional nurses. Determine in each situation whether the nurse was derelict in her duty to the patient and also whether, in your judgment, she demonstrated the level of foreseeabilty you would expect of a professional person.

Assessment—a necessary forerunner of foreseeability

FACTS. Bobbie Kerns was a very sick 8-year-old boy when he was admitted to the Emergency Room at St. Stephen's Hospital. His parents had recently moved to Center City and had not yet selected a family physician or pediatrician for Bobbie. He was seen by the intern on emergency room duty and then hospitalized under the care of Dr. Bizet.

Dr. Bizet saw Bobbie shortly after admission and prescribed a regimen that included antibiotic therapy, fluids, and oxygen if Bobbie became dyspneic. Because Bobbie was restless and frightened, hospital policy was waived and Bobbie's father was allowed to stay with him.

At 10:00 P.M., Mr. Kerns called the charge nurse, Edna Spock, to Bobbie's room. He was concerned because Bobbie seemed to be more restless and felt hot and dry. He asked that the physician be called and mentioned the fact that when Bobbie had pneumonia 2 years ago he had had a convulsion and the doctor had warned Mr. and Mrs. Kerns that it could happen again.

Edna took Bobbie's temperature and found it to be 102° F. (38.9° C.), an elevation of 2° since admission. Other than the rise in temperature, she observed no change in Bobbie's condition. She agreed to call the doctor and report the temperature rise, but she urged Mr. Kerns not to be unduly alarmed as children's temperatures often fluctuate rather dramatically.

After her telephone call to Dr. Bizet, Nurse Spock reported back to Mr. Kerns. The doctor concurred with her that there was at this point no cause for alarm. One hour later Bobbie had a severe seizure. A neurologic examination the following morning showed some weakness of the left arm and leg. Bobbie recovered from the pneumonia and left the hospital 2 weeks later with what was noted on his chart as "a neurological deficit involving the right arm and leg, probably due to a febrile seizure."

Subsequently, a suit was brought against St. Stephen's Hospital, Dr. Bizet, and Nurse Edna Spock charging negligence, resulting in the loss of normal use of Bobbie's right arm and leg.

ANALYSIS. St. Stephen's Hospital, Dr. Bizet, and Nurse Spock all enjoyed good reputations in their respective spheres in the health care system. All three obviously owed a legal duty to Bobbie. Why, then, did he come to harm?

The defense offered evidence supporting the fact that seizures in children of Bobbie's age are uncommon with temperature elevations of 102° F., and that the treatment regimen prescribed by Dr. Bizet and carried out by Edna Spock was adequate in view of the diagnosis and presenting symptoms. Doctor Bizet testified that he had not been told by either Bobbie's parents or the nurse that the patient had a prior history of febrile seizure. The most searching question asked was why had Edna Spock not listened to Mr. Kerns when he told her of Bobbie's previous seizure, or if she had listened, why had she not acted affirmatively to prevent such a reaction from occurring again. As an experienced pediatric nurse, she should have been aware that some children have low seizure thresholds and convulse with fevers as low as 100° to 102° F. (37.8° to 38.9° C.). Did she assume that since Bobbie had been seen by both an intern and a physician that his health history had been fully explored? Would such an assumption be reasonable? Does it imply that Edna sees herself, and nursing, in a dependent role with little or no duty to question or actively intervene once a medical regimen has been prescribed?

Patients, doctors, and hospitals rely on a professional nurse's judgment. They have a right to expect that, in arriving at that judgment, the nurse will draw on and relate her observations, the patient's health history, scientific fact, and empirical data. As a professional person, you, the reader, are in the best position to judge the conduct of Edna Spock. Was she or was she not derelict in her duty to Bobbie Kerns?

Nursing action that concealed nursing judgment

FACTS. Early in her career Rose Powers found that pediatric nursing was the area in which she could make the greatest contribution to nursing and to her own growth and development. Now Rose is an expert in her field and is recognized as such by her colleagues in both medicine and nursing.

Through years of experience, Rose had learned of the impending danger of convulsions in children with high fevers, and she had been dissatisfied with medical regimens that did not take this problem into account. In order to deal with this dissatisfaction, she developed a course of action that she applied on her own in virtually every situation. When a child had a high fever, she acted by giving a drug prescribed for pain that was both antipyretic and analgesic, although the child had neither objective nor subjective symptoms of pain. The patient's record would read, "aspirin gr iii given for pain," but Rose's intent was to reduce the child's fever. If an analgesic-antipyretic drug had not been ordered, she would give, under the guise of a bed bath, a tepid sponge bath to reduce fever.

Is Rose's conduct legal? Has she responded properly to her duty to the patient?

ANALYSIS. It is doubtful that Rose's conduct will ever bring harm to a patient, but is she not distorting facts and actually violating the law? She is administering a drug not for the stated purpose for which it was ordered, and she is administering a treatment without an order. Rose is unquestionably altering a medical regimen and substituting her own idea of what should be done. Furthermore she is doing it surreptitiously.

It is not suggested that Rose must challenge the physician by boldly stating that he is in error. What she needs to do is to stop playing games. She needs to sit down with the physician and discuss the problem, if need be, weighing her knowledge and experience against his. Together, then, they could use their combined wisdom in the best interest of the patient. Rose apparently understands she has a duty to the patient, and unlike Edna Spock in the previous situation, she foresees the harm that could come if she fails to act. However, she has gone outside the law to fulfill the duty and in concealing her action has failed to perform at a professional level. If Rose understood the legal significance of her actions, her conduct might well have taken a more purposeful direction.

Labeling of patients interferes with duty

FACTS. Heather Brown, a 17-year-old high school senior, was injured in a skiing accident. She sustained numerous contusions and bruises and simple fractures of the right tibia and fibula. Following the injury, she was admitted to the hospital. The fractures were reduced and a long leg cast applied.

Within a matter of days, Heather was out of bed on crutches. She worked hard to regain her mobility but was impeded by constant pain in her right leg. The pain persisted, but since frequent checks of the casted extremity gave no evidence of circulatory impairment, the physician and nursing staff concluded that Heather was "a baby" and the pain was probably psychological in origin.

After a week in which Heather became more frightened, frustrated, and antagonistic toward everyone, her parents asked for an orthopedic consultation. The cast was removed, and a diagnosis of foot drop owing to pressure on the peroneal nerve caused by improper padding in the area of the fibular head was made.

Physical therapy was prescribed and some function returned, but 1 year later Heather still wore a brace. Heather has not given up. From early childhood she has been a sports enthusiast and her goal has been to become a physical education teacher. Heather's treatment has been costly and her parents talk of suing. Heather, reluctant to accept her disability and convinced that she will fully recover, wants to forget past experiences and concentrate on getting well.

ANALYSIS. Whether or not a charge of negligence is brought against those who participated in Heather's care will be left to the Brown family. It should be useful, however, to consider the duty owed by the nursing staff and what part they played in the incident. It cannot be denied that from the time of Heather's admission to the nursing unit the staff owed her a legal duty. The question is, did their conduct measure up to what one would expect of a reasonably prudent professional nurse in the exercise of that duty?

As has been explained, the nurses did examine the casted extremity for circulatory impairment, the usual cause of pain. They reported their findings and the patient's complaint to the attending physician. Did their duty end there? Or, since the pain persisted, were they negligent in labeling Heather's behavior and concurring in the opinion that the pain was psychologic without taking action that would affirm or rule out an organic basis for pain? Had they really come to know Heather as a person, would this labeling have occurred and would they not have been more aggressive in seeking other reasons for the pain? Regardless of the origin of the pain, it would seem that little was done by the nursing staff to support the patient.

Although none of the nursing staff was present when the cast was applied or in a position to judge the skill with which it was applied, they all knew pain persisted following its application, and that it could not be attributed to general circulatory impairment. Certainly, it is within the expertise of a professional nurse to suspect nerve damage when pain in a casted extremity persists. Furthermore, it is within the legal duty of the nurse to act positively to prevent further damage even though that action was without the support or contrary to the orders of the patient's physician. Therefore it seems logical to conclude that the nursing staff owed Heather a legal duty and, in exercising that duty, failed to foresee harm and to act affirmatively in safeguarding her well-being.

Summary

In the situations cited the legal duty owed the patient was closely tied to the nurses' ability to foresee harm and to act with conviction to allay that harm. The knowledge necessary to prevent harm from occurring was easily within the grasp of today's professional nurse.

If nursing is to hold its position in a developing health care system, it can be expected that greater demands will be placed on its practitioners. To meet these demands, the knowledge base must be enlarged, the process of decision making facilitated, and the autonomy of the nurse preserved. The nurse who has begun to integrate law into the nursing process has taken one firm step toward meeting the challenge of tomorrow. Recognition of the legal duty owed another and the obligation to see that person is not harmed are basic to the supporting structure of any service profession.

6

Causation

Modern health care in a broad sense is a complex system with many interacting parts. Within each part, health care personnel with divergent backgrounds and different orientations work toward the common goal of improving the health of individuals, families, and communities. In an emergency situation the paramedic squad may have the task of sustaining life and transporting a patient to a hospital. The emergency room physician and nurses have the obligation of providing life-supporting, immediate care. The attending physician, staff nurses, and other health professionals, such as physical therapists and nutritionists, have the duty to restore the patient to health. Finally, public health personnel facilitate the individual's return to the community. Thus health is restored by the coordinated interaction of numerous facets in the health care system.

A less favorable side of this united effort is seen when there is a breakdown in the care being given, at any level or stage, that leads to harm or actual injury to the patient. Another way to put this issue, and one that is the subject of this chapter, is that action or inaction on the part of any person on the health care team, may "cause" injury to the patient.

Given the complexity of the etiology of disease and the many factors that could contribute to an injury, it may often not be apparent which member or members of the health team "caused" the injury, of if, in fact, the injury that actually occurred to the patient may not have been "caused" by the conduct of any member of the health team but may have been the result of a product used in giving care. Nonetheless, the issue of causation in any legal analysis of accountability is fundamental.

The previous chapters have discussed the measurement of a health care professional's obligation and the formulation of his legal duty. Falling below these standards, or breaching a duty, may give rise to legal accountability in the event an injury occurs. However, each dereliction of duty or each instance of substandard care does not give rise to legal liability. It is only when such conduct or misconduct *causes,* that is, leads to, injury to the patient that liability may be found. *Substandard care or a breach of duty does not lead to liability unless a causal relationship can be established between the one or ones giving the care and the injury claimed. In other words, a connecting link between the two must be found in order to justify a claim of negligence.*

PROOF OF CAUSATION—RELEVANT VARIABLES

Proof of a causal relationship between the conduct of the health care professional and the injury that occurred is frequently difficult. Often the blurring of functions and diffusion of responsibilities within a health care system makes it impossible to hold any one person accountable for a single act of patient care. Failure to establish evidence of a causal relationship, either through direct testimony or through the opinion evidence of a health care expert, may mean that, although there is no dispute that the injury was sustained, the case is lost for want of evidence that the defendant, the one accused, was the one who brought about the harm.

For example, hypothesize that a patient suffered an unfavorable drug reaction. Was the cause of harm an error on the part of the physician who ordered the drug, the substandard conduct of the nurse who administered the drug, the fault of the manufacturer who prepared the drug, or an unpredictable response on the part of the patient who received the drug?

Financial responsibility for the harm that has occurred cannot be fairly imposed until a causal relationship can be found. The law has attempted to find a solution to this problem by devising various tests, and the one in common usage today is called the *substantial factor test.*

In nursing practice there are many instances in which there can be no certainties other than the exercise of one's best judgment; so too in law. The law does not demand certainty to find a causal link between actions and injury. For example, should harm come to a patient, it is only necessary to show that a nurse's negligent conduct was a substantial factor contributing to the harm in order to impose legal and financial responsibility. It need not be the sole causative agent, and indeed it may not even be the principal cause. For nurses to be held liable, it is sufficient that their conduct has contributed substantially to the harm that has occurred. This does not preclude the possibility that others could also be found liable.

The substantial factor test is a particularly important concept in analyzing an incident that involves the interactions of a number of health professionals in giving service to a patient. It may not be easy to say which one, if any, of the individuals breached a duty leading to the injury; what is clear is that someone has been harmed and that the responsibility might have been shared.

The community health nurse who operates in a setting that provides only limited contact with a physician often must make judgments and act with little or no colleague support. In the instance in which a decision to act was made after a telephone consultation with a physician and harm came to the patient because of the action, it would be necessary to establish whether the physician's concurrence was a substantial factor in causing the harm. While both physician and nurse may have opinions as to their responsibilities, it would be the role of the court to determine the point at which the care broke down and whether the conduct of either or both was a substantial factor in causing the harm.

FIXING RESPONSIBILITIES IN MULTIPLE CAUSATION

In instances of alleged negligence in health care settings, it is not often that a single defendant can be said to be the one, and only one, who brought about the harm. Complex team relationships and interagency involvement in the delivery of health care frequently can lead to questions of multiple causation when an injury occurs. A number of suits may follow. In each one the problem of proof is a complicated legal process for it is necessary to present factual evidence to show that the negligent conduct of the one, or ones, accused was the immediate cause of the harm.

In the following case, note how the possibility of multiple causation can so cloud the evidence that the conduct of any single actor cannot be shown to have been a substantial factor in bringing about the harm.[6]

The plaintiff, Mrs. Brown, went to Shannon Hospital in response to a request for blood donors. At this time an arrangement was in effect whereby Baylor University furnished supplies for the blood donations and, after Shannon Hospital collected the blood, it was returned to Baylor University for processing and distribution.

At the time of Mrs. Brown's phlebotomy some difficulty was encountered in inserting the needle into her vein. Following the procedure she complained of constant pain in the area, was hospitalized several times, and was treated by a number of physicians for cellulitis originating in the antecubital space of the involved arm. Ultimately, Mrs. Brown brought suit against Shannon Hospital charging that the use of a nonsterile needle was the proximate cause of injury.

That Mrs. Brown had sustained a serious injury was not disputed. One medical expert testified ". . . it's safe to assume there's some type of chronic infection . . . there's an obvious contracture of the elbow and . . . a shortening of the muscles so that I don't believe she can extend this arm."

The plaintiff, however, lost the case for failure to prove Shannon Hospital and its nurses were at fault. Shannon claimed, in its defense, that the break in aseptic technique could have occurred at Baylor University when the supplies were packaged. Expert testimony held that it was impossible to state the source of an infection or the point at which it occurred. In fact, it was possible the onset of the infection may not have been due to the procedure, and the harm may not have been due to the negligent conduct of either Shannon Hospital or Baylor University.

This case illustrates that when a given result may have more than one proximate cause, the jury may be left with conjecture instead of factual evidence on which to base its decision. There is no easy route in seeking a causal relationship when an injury occurs. Causation usually has to be determined on the basis of facts surrounding the incident plus mixed considerations of logic, common sense, justice, policy, and precedent.

PRODUCTS LIABILITY

Injury to those receiving services in various areas of the delivery of health care may arise from ways other than failure of any member of the health care team to provide an accepted standard of care. When injury occurs through no fault of the one giving the care, then another causal relationship plainly has entered the picture. A not infrequent cause of harm is the failure of any one of the numerous products used in rendering health care services. When such injuries do occur, the nurse practitioner may be directly involved as the one who actually used the product or who participated in its use as a member of the health team.

It must be emphasized that products can be defective and give rise to an injury even though they are handled properly and professionally in every respect. Manufacturing defects may not be discovered by visual examination or through a knowledge of the product's constituents. Under a law known as the Federal Food, Drug and Cosmetic Act,[7] quality standards are set for medical products. Under the quality control provisions of this Act, medical devices ranging all the way from bandages and tongue depressors to pacemakers and heart and lung machines are regulated. Quality controls on "critical devices" such as IUDs (intrauterine devices), artificial blood vessels, heart valve replacements, and respirators are very strict and even extend to building maintenance, personnel training, record keeping, equipment design, packaging, and labeling. Moreover, the manufacturer, in addition to observing the above quality controls, must demonstrate—usually through extensive testing—that the product indeed is efficacious and achieves the effect for which it is marketed.

If an injury arises because of a defective product or piece of equipment, the manufacturer is immediately exposed to liability. The legal doctrine that imposes such liability is generally termed "products liability." The term "products liability" does not lend itself to a simplistic definition. The scope of the manufacturer's legal responsibility is vast. However, a causal relationship between a product and an injury may be difficult to establish in view of other possible causal factors.

It is not sufficient to impose legal responsibility to show that the injury arises from use of the product. It must also be shown that the product was defective as manufactured, and that it was the defect that caused the injury. Thus, in an automobile accident case, it may be shown that the headlights were defective; but, if the accident occurred during daylight hours, there would be no causal relationship between the accident and the defective headlights. Similarly, injury may follow a dynamite explosion; but, unless the dynamite can be proven to be defective, no responsibility exists on the part of the maker.

The liability that arises, when harm can be claimed, is for the manufacturer, sometimes the distributor, but clearly not the user. For example, if a patient with an external pacemaker connected to a pacing catheter in the heart experienced ventricular fibrillation caused by leakage of current from a defective electric bed, the manufacturer of the bed and/or the hospital that provided the bed for the patient might be liable for the injury sustained by the patient.

FAILURE TO WARN

A product may be defective, through faulty components or faulty assembly, but the manufacturer's responsibility goes much further. He is also responsible for the information that accompanies the product. He must tell the consumer how to use the product, under what conditions it may be used, and what the potential hazards are, related to its use.

Common experience, as well as medical training, teaches that products in general cannot be made entirely safe. Knives cut, matches burn, drugs have side effects, and so on. No responsibility, therefore, can fairly be imposed upon the manufacturer or seller of products merely because injuries are caused thereby. The law has, however, seen fit to impose a duty over and above the duty to supply a nondefective product, and that is the duty to provide a warning of the dangers inherent in the product. The familiar package insert on drugs constitutes an attempt by the manufacturers of such drugs to warn of the risks of utilization of the product. Analogous to the duty of disclosure placed upon health practitioners discussed in Chapter 10, the duty to disclose the potential consequences of using a product rests with the manufacturer. Thus, in the drug context, a manufacturer will typically be required to conduct a series of animal tests concerning the efficacy and side effects of the drugs. If, in the course of such testing, significant risks are perceived, and significant areas of potential side effects are known, they must be the subject of a warning. Obviously, a judgment must be made by the patient as to whether the benefits derived from the use of a particular product outweigh the potential harm that could result; but the patient's decision must be based on full disclosure by both the manufacturer and the attending medical practitioners. For example, a patient with osteoporosis must be fully informed before he can measure the benefits of taking an estrogen preparation as a deterrent to further vertebral deterioration against the potential risk of developing cancer from the possible carcinogenic effect associated with its long-term use.

The responsibility of the manufacturer to disseminate information and to warn of risks can be more difficult to manage than the actual production of the product. Who should be warned? The distributor? The consumer? Others? What constitutes adequate warning? How does the manufacturer capture the attention of the physician, the professional nurse, or other health-care givers? Does a particular warning adequately communicate the gravity of dangers, or does it gloss over its warning to promote the sales of a product? Is it a danger the manufacturer knows, or should know, and one the user would not ordinarily discover? To what extent can the manufacturer of a drug or other medical product be expected to provide a warning that is adequate for a consumer population with widely divergent cultural and intellectual characteristics?

One of the far-reaching and perhaps surprising principles in products liability is the fact that a manufacturer may be held to a duty to warn of risks or problems of which he was not aware and which could not be predicted or foreseen by the use of known techniques—for example, the cases that hold hospitals liable for the supply of blood for transfusions, which sometimes give rise to hepatitis in the recipient. There is no known way to screen blood for the existence of the hepatitis-causing agent; but, nonetheless, in many states, hospitals are liable for the resulting disease in the event the contaminated blood is used.

DRUG LIABILITY

A very important area in which products liability arises within a medical context is in the use of drugs; much litigation has arisen from various marketed pharmaceutical products. As, however, a leading government official pointed out:

> There is no such thing as absolute safety in drugs. There are some drugs that are less liable to cause harmful reaction than others, but people die every year from drugs generally regarded as innocuous.[8]

Drug injuries can be divided into various categories: (1) toxic reactions, which are dose-related and predictable; (2) hypersensitivity and allergic reactions, which may or may not be generally predictable; (3) completely idiosyncratic reactions; and (4) tetratogenic reactions. Generally, the suits involving drugs take one of two forms. Either the drug is alleged to be defective, or it is claimed that the manufacturer has failed to warn of the dangers inherent in its use.

Examples of current drug litigation that have assumed significant proportions include litigation based upon the use of birth control pills and the administration of various vaccines. In the instance of *Reyes v. Wyeth Laboratories*,[9] 8-month old Anita Reyes was given a trivalent oral polio vaccine and became completely paralyzed. The parents contended that the manufacturer had failed to warn them of the dangers. The vaccine, known as the Sabin vaccine, was made up of living but attenuated organisms.

There was a warning on the package that accompanied the vials of vaccine when it was sold to the Texas State Health Department. The public health nurse in the clinic gave the vaccine. She testified in court that she had read the warning insert, but it was not a practice to pass the warning on to the parents or the guardians. The court, however, said that the manufacturer did indeed have the obligation to see that a warning was given, but not directly to the parents.

The defense contended that Anita's paralysis was not caused by the vaccine but, rather, was a part of a polio epidemic prevalent in the community at the time. The jury rejected the contention of the defense. An award of $200,000 was upheld.

In view of the fact that it is usually the clinic or office nurse who administers immunizing agents, this decision should cause nurses to consider the extent of their professional and legal responsibility for disclosure relative to immunization programs in general. Have nurses exercised professional responsibility for informing consumers regarding benefits and risks associated with a particular immunizing agent? Might they, in a situation similar to the Reyes incident, be held legally accountable for not communicating the manufacturer's warning to the client/patient? In fact, it is the duty of professional nurses to incorporate into their patient teaching any known risks associated with the drug being administered, in a manner consistent with the medical requirements of disclosure.

Numerous other examples exist of controversies in drug litigation as to whether the manufacturer knew or had reason to suspect that certain side effects were indeed caused by the product (for example, whether strokes in any given case could be caused by birth control pills). In the case of *Mahr v. G.D. Searle & Co.*,[10] the husband of the deceased sued Searle & Co. for the wrongful death of his wife based on a prescription for an oral contraceptive. The plaintiff claimed that the drug was dispensed without adequate warning of possible adverse side effects. Ms. Mahr was a young and healthy woman until she started taking the drug. She then had several clotting episodes, blackouts, and dizzy spells; after a stroke, she died of an occlusion of the left internal carotid artery. The court found the manufacturer liable because it had failed to provide an adequate warning of foreseeable adverse consequences, and that malpractice of the physician, if any, would not relieve the manufacturer of responsibility.

Focusing on the manufacturer's responsibility, the courts reaffirmed the right of the patient to be warned of foreseeable adverse consequences.

Again, this decision suggests that nurses must consider what their role should be in relation to reinforcing or initiating disclosure relative to drug therapy.

NURSING ROLE IN PRODUCTS LIABILITY

There are several possible ways in which nurses in their practice interact with products liability matters. They may be observers in terms of analyzing symptoms or problems, as in the case of drug side effects. They may be participants in the unwitting use of defective equipment. They may likewise be participants in an injury-causing situation in which it is ambiguous as to whether their conduct led to the injury or whether a defective product was involved. They may be called on to give care to a patient hospitalized for an injury from a defective product. Finally, they may occasionally be the victims themselves, if they are injured through defective products in the course of their professional activities.

Some questions arise in seeking a causal relationship when both the conduct of the nurse and a product are under examination. The manufacturer may contend that the defect was created by the alteration of the product or that harm was a consequence of misuse of the product rather than a defect. Consider the responsibility of the manufacturer or the professional nurse should the nurse recognize that the solution in the syringe appeared to have undergone a slight precipitation but, in haste, ignored this observation and administered the injection. If the patient suffered harm, who might be held liable, the manufacturer, the nurse, or both?

The case of *Richard v. Southwest Louisiana Hospital Association*[11] further illustrates how a health care facility and its professional employees can become legally involved when harm follows the use of a defective product.

During a period of hospitalization following a fracture of the right leg, the patient, Richard, had difficulty voiding. A catheter was inserted for several days, after which he developed a stricture of the urethral canal. When other means to relieve the stricture were unsuccessful, a "patch urethroplasty" was performed, during which a Foley catheter was inserted. On the third postoperative day, the patient suffered a bladder spasm, which caused the catheter to dislodge, permitting urine to pass over the surgical area, adversely affecting the healing process. Later, it was determined that the Foley catheter balloon had a minute leak. The patient underwent two more surgical procedures over a period of several months and was left with some residual damage.

Richard sued the hospital, its employees, and the manufacturer of the catheter. The suit against the manufacturer was dropped when it could not be established which one of several manufacturers had furnished the hospital with the catheter. The sole determining factor in the suit then became the charge that the hospital, through its employees, was negligent in failing to test the catheter for leaks prior to its use. Since it was the duty of the hospital to protect its patients from external circumstances within its control, had the hospital breached its duty to Richard?

Both nurses and doctors testified for the hospital that, when reusable Foley catheters were furnished by the hospital to the patient, it had been the then-standard practice to test the balloon before insertion. With the introduction of prepackaged, sterile, disposable catheters, the practice of testing was discontinued. Moreover, the product literature did not recommend testing, nor did it state that it should not be done. Medical testimony also pointed out that, to discover such a small leak, the catheter balloon would have to have been overdistended and that this much pressure could have weakened the balloon prior to the catheter's use. An expert witness, a nurse from a local university, was called to give an opinion on two textbooks on bedside nursing techniques, which were admitted into evidence. She testified that the author of the texts was a competent authority on the subject of nursing techniques and that the texts reflected current practice. Neither text distinguished between reusable and disposable catheters from the standpoint of pretesting the balloon. Nonetheless, the plaintiff was awarded $81,000 because the hospital had used a defective catheter and should have known of its defect.

As seen in this case, the responsibility of a health care agency to protect the patient from external circumstances within its control is one that must be given serious attention by professional nurses.

PRODUCTS LIABILITY—ONE FACTOR IN THE TOTAL FIELD OF CAUSAL RELATIONSHIPS

Since professional nurses today often occupy central positions in the management of patient care, their responsibility may expand to include the inspection and proper maintenance of highly technical equipment, as well as the duty to keep themselves and others informed as to new, innovative techniques and therapeutic interventions. Professional nurses draw on a knowledge of the basic sciences to ensure that the obligation to protect the patient is met. Continuing education and a thorough assessment and evaluation of each patient situation are safeguards that serve to minimize the possibility that patient harm may result from either employee conduct or any product used in the patient's care.

Today, patients, particularly those with chronic diseases, are being given a new lease on life through the use of sophisticated equipment and/ or complex drug therapy. Examples of this are seen in the patient with chronic renal disease on a home dialysis program and the transplant patient whose welfare rests on strict adherence to a drug regimen. Because of their relationship to the patient, nurses are often the health professionals best qualified to assume the task of preparing the patient for life outside a health care facility and of supporting him and his family as he reestablishes himself in the community. To do so, nurses must be able to acquaint the patient with any dangers inherent in the product or regimen on which he is dependent in a way that is understandable and nonthreatening. This task demands not only expertise in the art of communication, but also a thorough knowledge of the patient, his disease, and the product's potential for good or harm.

The field of products liability related to drugs and equipment used in preventive, therapeutic, and rehabilitative care should be of great interest to the professional nurse practitioner. Both the manufacturer and the health care giver share a responsibility, and it is never easy to determine the point at which the legal accountability of each begins and ends. Neither is it always possible to isolate the effect of a product from other variables entering into a causal relationship. The nurse who is aware that harm can arise from many sources has taken the first step in providing safe patient care.

RES IPSA LOQUITUR

To this point discussion has centered on the fact that in order to fix legal liability it is necessary to prove a causal relationship between the injury that occurred and the negligent conduct of the one accused of bringing it about. Specific negligent conduct must be established by factual evidence and must be shown to have been a substantial factor in bringing about the alleged injury.

We turn briefly to the legal doctrine of *res ipsa loquitur,* a Latin phrase meaning "the thing speaks for itself." The term thus describes a situation in which the harm that occurred is so blatant it can readily be presumed such harm would not or could not occur in the absence of negligence. Ordinarily, the plaintiff accuses the defendant of bringing about the harm, and the burden of proof is his continuing responsibility. In those instances when the doctrine of *res ipsa loquitur* is invoked, the process is reversed and the plaintiff is called on to demonstrate only (1) that the injury was a kind that ordinarily does not occur in the absence of negligence, (2) that the injury was caused by an instrumentality or agency within the exclusive control of the defendant, and (3) that the injury could not have been due to any voluntary action on the part of the plaintiff.

Consider these three conditions in light of a charge of negligence made by a patient who after undergoing a thoracotomy found that a needle had been left in his chest. Although it could be said that this was an unlikely incident, still it could not be viewed as the hand of Providence; it definitely gave rise to a presumption of negligence. It could also be said that the instrumentality was in the hands of the operating room staff, and that the patient was unconscious and could not have contributed in any way to what happened.

Health care practitioners tend to view the doctrine of *res ipsa loquitur* as a legal maneuver that could place them on the defensive for every unfavorable result even though an inference of negligence is unfounded. Obviously, certain circumstances surrounding the injury dictate whether or not the doctrine can be reasonably applied. For example, if a patient with metastatic bone cancer was discovered to have a fracture of the spine following transfer from his bed to a chair, it would be difficult to support a charge of negligence, for it could be said that the injury was one that might occur under conditions of careful handling.

Controversy exists as to whether the doctrine of *res ipsa loquitur* as applied to medical malpractice has been extended beyond its original purpose to the point of becoming a "rule of sympathy": meaning that the injured one has the sympathy of the court and that an inference of negligence follows too easily. If this point of view is accepted, then every unfavorable result could put the health care practitioner in the position of having to prove that circumstances, which were actually beyond his control, were not negligent acts. One can easily see the legal quandary for the professional nurse should decubitus ulcers occur in an elderly malnourished patient or should a patient experience an unexpected drug reaction. However, those who favor its application contend that a person who sustains an injury is entitled to reasonable legal means to secure redress for that injury.

In the case of *Ybarra v. Spangard,*[12] the court upheld the right of the plaintiff to invoke the doctrine of *res ipsa loquitur.* The plaintiff, Ybarra, underwent an appendectomy performed by Dr. Spangard in a hospital owned and operated by Dr. Swift. Ybarra testified that he was pulled up on the operating table and laid back against two hard objects at the top of his shoulders. On awakening from the anesthetic he complained of a sharp pain in his right shoulder. Prior to this operation he had never suffered any pain in or injury to his shoulder. The pain persisted and, in fact, worsened after his release from the hospital, eventually leading to paralysis and atrophy of the shoulder muscle.

Ybarra filed suit, naming as defendants Dr. Spangard and other physicians and nurses who participated in the surgical procedure and in his postoperative care.

The defendants contended that (1) where there was a division of responsibility in the use of the instrumentality causing the injury, the rule of *res ipsa loquitur* could not be invoked; and (2) the plaintiff had not shown which of several instrumentalities that he came in contact with had caused the injury or that any one defendant had exclusive control over any instrumentality.

> The court determined that "the number of those in whose care a patient is placed is not a good reason for denying him all reasonable opportunity to recovery for negligent harm . . . that where a plaintiff receives unusual injuries while unconscious and in the course of medical treatment, all those defendants who had any control over his body or the instrumentalities which might have caused the injuries may properly be called upon to meet the inference of negligence by giving an explanation of their conduct."

In such situations where the patient was unconscious and it is not possible for him to obtain direct proof of negligence, the doctrine of *res ipsa loquitur* places the defendant in the position of explaining why what happened did happen. Thus it provides a means by which an injured patient may have his day in court.

WHEN NURSING ACTION CAUSES HARM

Even though today's nurse does not subscribe to the traditional "Angel of Mercy" image, all nurses take well-deserved pride in the fact that theirs is a helping profession. The care functions of nursing generally have high priority in any assessment of nursing's uniqueness.

This orientation probably makes it more difficult for nurses to be objectively analytical in examining their own or a colleague's conduct, particularly when they must seek a causal relationship between what nurses did or did not do to bring about harm to another. Unpleasant as this task may be, it is essential if nursing is to safeguard its practice and to grow in its appreciation of the nature of its relationship to other health workers.

In the hypothetical situations that follow, use the previously described test of causation to evaluate nurse involvement and determine the critical point at which the alleged harm could have been avoided through alternative courses of action.

The action of Nurse Bowers as a cause of injury

FACTS. Mrs. Kate Amter was a frequent patient on the gynecologic service at Lancaster General Hospital. Her symptoms were generally elusive and transitory in nature and had earned for her the unofficial diagnosis of hypochondriasis. Most recently she had been admitted for biopsy of a breast tumor, which proved to be benign.

As usual, Mrs. Amter's convalescence was slow. She was reluctant to ambulate and complained of constant pain and tenderness in the operative site. On the morning of the sixth postoperative day her physician discontinued all medication and told her that he would probably discharge her later in the day after he had talked with the surgeon.

Mrs. Amter continued to complain of pain, refused her lunch, and insisted that her doctor be called. The team leader, Judy Bowers, called the surgeon, who ordered 10 grains of aspirin and gave his approval for Mrs. Amter's discharge.

When Nurse Bowers brought the medication to the bedside, Mrs. Amter said, "If that's aspirin I can't take it. My doctor knows I'm allergic." Judy responded, "Of course he knows what you can take. This will give you a good rest before you get ready to go home." Mrs. Amter took the drug.

About a half hour later, a nurse's aide reported that Mrs. Amter was having trouble breathing and seemed very frightened. Nurse Bowers went to Mrs. Amter's room and immediately recognized that the patient was experiencing a severe anaphylactic reaction. The house physician was called, an antihistamine and adrenaline were administered, but it was necessary to perform a tracheostomy to establish an adequate airway.

Mrs. Amter recovered and brought suit against the Lancaster General Hospital and Judy Bowers, charging negligence that had resulted in a tracheostomy and subsequent pain and disfigurement.

ANALYSIS. If it were not for the administration of two aspirin tablets, Mrs. Amter would have left Lancaster General Hospital following her physician's afternoon rounds instead of undergoing the traumatic experience that she did.

In carrying out a physician's drug order, which was certainly not in itself questionable, was Nurse Bowers negligent? If one looks only at the act of administering a drug to a patient who at the time exhibited no remarkable symptoms it would seem to be acceptable conduct. However, since a professional nurse knows, or should know, the serious nature of a systemic response to an allergen, and that aspirin, while an innocuous drug in most cases, has been known to induce life-threatening anaphylactic reactions, any reference made by a patient to such allergy should have been heeded.

Undoubtedly the fact that Mrs. Amter had the reputation of being a difficult patient, prone to symptoms that could not be medically verified, caused Judy to take lightly the patient's claim that she could not take aspirin. Judy did not deny that the drug was aspirin but in avoiding the question led the patient to believe that it was not.

Nurse Bowers acted efficiently and with dispatch in handling a drug reaction that could have proved fatal to the patient. However, had she not ignored the patient's warning and administered the drug, the reaction and its related trauma would not have occurred. From the facts cited, it is likely that the court would approve a finding that Nurse Bowers' conduct was a substantial factor in causing the harm Mrs. Amter experienced.

Diet, a substantial factor in the therapeutic regimen

FACTS. David, a student nurse, was assigned to care for Melanie, age 7. Melanie had been hospitalized for 1 week with a diagnosis of acute glomerulonephritis. During that week her condition had worsened with continuing rise in blood pressure, increasing edema, and diminishing urinary output.

In reviewing her history and treatment regimen, David was struck by the fact that Melanie was on a 5-gram sodium diet. In team conference he questioned the diet order in view of the progression of symptoms. The team leader was unable to explain the rationale for the order but reminded David that there were different theories relative to the dietary management of acute glomerulonephritis.

David then discussed the diet order with his instructor who agreed that it would be reasonable to expect greater sodium restriction, since 5 grams was within the average normal daily intake. She advised him to discuss the matter with Melanie's physician, Dr. Broom.

Dr. Broom arrived just as Melanie's lunch was served. David met him at the nurses' station and broached the subject of sodium restriction for Melanie. Dr. Broom said he thought a 500-mg restriction was sufficient. David pointed out that Melanie was on a 5-gram (5000-mg) sodium diet now. A stormy discussion followed involving the head nurse, team leader, unit secretary, and Dr. Broom. The original order was reviewed. Dr. Broom's handwriting was difficult to decipher, and the decimal point that he insisted preceded "5-gram" was only vaguely discernible. Dr. Broom angrily protested that any responsible person would have realized that he meant 0.5-gram (500-mg), even though his handwriting left much to be desired. He demanded that Melanie's tray be returned to the kitchen and that the diet order be changed immediately. Melanie's mother asked why, and Dr. Broom explained that he had just discovered Melanie was getting too much salt. Melanie's mother asked if that was why her blood pressure had been rising. Dr. Broom said it could have been the reason.

Later in the day Melanie's mother told David that she was going to talk to her lawyer. She felt strongly that someone had been negligent and that Melanie had been the victim.

ANALYSIS. Since Melanie recovered with no apparent complications, no legal action was instituted. If, however, she had shown evidence of renal or cardiac failure or of central nervous system involvement, damages from negligence could well have been claimed.

Since dietary modification is recognized as an important measure in the treatment of acute glomerulonephritis, lack of due care in providing a proper dietary regimen could be the basis for a charge of negligence. Although it would be difficult to prove that any complication was directly or solely due to an error in dietary management, it could be argued that such an error could have been a substantial factor in bringing about harm.

In this instance the responsibility for the harm that might have occurred would have, in all probability, been shared. The physician who wrote the order and the professional nurses, who, over a period of 1 week, observed the progressive decline of their patient without seriously assessing the total situation, failed in their duty to provide for Melanie an acceptable standard of care.

The injury speaks of negligence

FACTS. Carl Ward, a 42-year-old accountant, was admitted to Cramer General Hospital for open-heart surgery necessitating total cardiopulmonary bypass. Prior to surgery he was given a thorough physical examination and orientation to the postoperative regimen that would follow.

The surgical procedure was accomplished successfully, and Carl was transported to the intensive care unit where he was comatose for 24 hours. In general, however, the postoperative course was uneventful. Carl's condition, as expected, necessitated continuous skilled nursing care. Gradually, his vital signs stabilized, and he began to become involved in his surroundings.

On the third postoperative day he complained of a "scratchy" feeling in his right eye. The irritation became increasingly painful, and 2 days later an eye examination revealed an abrasion and ulceration of the cornea. Cortisone and antibiotic therapy was initiated, and Carl was advised that he should remain under the care of an ophthalmologist and that he could expect some loss of vision from corneal scarring.

Carl was very concerned about the possible loss of vision. He felt that, should it occur, it would interfere with his ability to function in his job with the same degree of effectiveness as he did prior to surgery. Although he fully appreciated that his overall health had been restored through the skill exercised by the cardiac surgery team and the intensive care nurses, he believes that the corneal injury could only be attributed to an error on someone's part. He is considering a charge of negligence and has sought the advice of his attorney.

ANALYSIS. A possible avenue for Carl to recover damages for his loss of vision is the doctrine of *res ipsa loquitur*. This would place the burden of proof on the defendant, since it is virtually impossible for the patient to fix specific blame for the trauma to his right cornea. However, if he can establish through medical testimony that such a corneal abrasion would occur only as a result of negligence, it is logical then to assume that the damage occurred during the prolonged period he was under anesthesia or during the coma that followed. This conclusion is reinforced by the fact that the intensive physical assessment prior to surgery elicited no corneal abrasion or defect. In the absence of protective corneal reflexes, it is possible that some irritant solution was inadvertently introduced into the eye or that a carelessly handled drape or bed sheet scraped the cornea—instrumentalities that could have been within the control of the anesthesiologist, operating room personnel, or the intensive care staff. Whatever the instrumentality causing the injury, it can be presumed that failure to protect the eyes of the anesthetized or comatose patient does not measure up to an acceptable standard of care and therefore could be said to be negligent conduct. Furthermore, the probability of Carl contributing voluntarily to the act is almost inconceivable, and his right to recover seems warranted should loss of vision ensue.

Product liability affects nursing care

FACTS. Barstow Hospital is a 500-bed general hospital located in a thriving industrial community. Three years ago, in order to deal more effectively with the needs of its patient population, hospital administration established an intravenous therapy department. Presently, the department is staffed on a 24-hour basis with professional nurses who have been given advanced preparation and supervised practice in the administration of intravenous fluids and medications.

The department has functioned effectively under the supervision of Elaine Warwick, R.N., who had been given full responsibility for the selection of supplies and equipment. Two months ago, the hospital purchasing agent recommended to administration that, in the interest of economy, future purchases for the intravenous department should be made from Failsafe Medical Products rather than the company that had been supplying the department for the past 3 years. The purchasing agent's recommendation was accepted without consultation with the supervisor or staff of the intravenous department.

No sooner had the change been effected than the department was flooded with calls from nurses on patient care units, complaining of problems associated with intravenous administration. Adaptors were inadequate, which often resulted in wasted fluids and drenched patients. Filters did not function properly, which allowed air bubbles to enter the patient's vein. Difficulty was encountered in maintaining a steady flow rate, causing patients to receive more or less of a drug in a prescribed period of time. These complaints were reported by both the intravenous department staff and unit nurses to the hospital administrator, where they were summarily dismissed as ungrounded.

Realizing the potential for harm in the situation, Elaine Warwick developed a plan whereby she could present the administrator with irrefutable evidence. A careful record of all complaints was kept, including the time spent by both the department staff and unit nurses in coping with the problem, as well as an exact account of the problem and its effect on the patient care regimen. In addition, all defective equipment was returned to the intravenous department as evidence of its inadequacy. It is expected that, armed with this concrete data, Ms. Warwick's voice will be heard.

ANALYSIS. One can certainly appreciate today the need to reduce the cost of health care, but not at risk to the patient or by lowering the standard of care. In the event that harm does come to a patient receiving intravenous therapy with defective equipment, it is quite likely that Failsafe Medical Products, Barstow Hospital, and professional nurses who initiated the therapy and who were responsible for its continued supervision might all become embroiled in legal proceedings. Even if the manufacturer were found to be liable for its product, the hospital or nurses would not necessarily be free from blame.

Although the professional nurses involved recognized the inherent danger in using Failsafe supplies and equipment, their foreseeability, unfortunately, did not prevent the continued use of an unsatisfactory product. It is certainly doubtful that a court would view their conduct as meeting an acceptable standard of care.

The action taken by Elaine Warwick in accumulating data to support the nurses' position is commendable. It demonstrates an organized approach to a difficult institutional problem, a recognition of the extent of professional responsibility, and, most importantly, a concern for the safety and welfare of the patient.

Summary

The determination of causal relationships between an act or acts and the harm that follows is a matter for the courts. It is, however, of prime importance for nurses, as they go about the daily practice of nursing, to evaluate all patient responses and to search for the most logical reason for their occurrence. In this way they are in a position to judge what is effective and what is not effective, or even harmful, in the patient care regimen.

A better understanding of the significance of causal relationships should lead nurses to assess more critically all factors that could contribute to negative or injurious responses. Then, through either avoiding harm or eliminating unproductive therapies, the quality of care could be upgraded and health restored at less cost to the patient and to society.

7

The professional nurse as a witness

Accountability for independent nursing practice has led professional nurses to rethink and redefine the knowledge and skills necessary to deliver the quality of nursing care expected of them. In line with this increased accountability is a correspondingly increased probability that they will be asked to interpret to the court the components of quality nursing care. They may be asked to give an account of the care actually given, or to give an opinion from the facts of the litigation under consideration as to whether the nursing conduct reported met the standard of care expected of a professional nurse.

As litigation in personal injuries relating to health care increases in frequency, there is an increasing need for the professional nurse to give thought to competency in the evaluation of the quality of nursing care. This is particularly true when the conduct of the nurse and/or the physician is being questioned. Medical and nursing practice today are so commingled that, not infrequently, both the professional nurse and the physician may be alleged to be legally responsible for having contributed to the same harm.

In most instances, neither the professional nurse nor the physician can answer for the other. The role of the physician is primarily one of diagnosing and determining appropriate intervention, some of which he carries out and a large part of which is delegated to other health professionals. Although physicians are continually assessing a treatment regimen, their actual contact with the patient is limited. In contrast, the nurse is with the patient for longer periods of time, and therefore has more opportunity to assess the continuum of care. Nursing functions fall into three categories:

those initiated and carried out independently by the nurse; those delegated by another member of the health team; and those derived by collaboration with other members of the health team. If, under any of these circumstances, the nursing conduct is questioned, it is logical to assume that a nurse rather than a physician is best qualified to judge whether or not the conduct met an acceptable standard of care.

Today's professional nurse is being held legally accountable as never before. Current nurse practice acts are identifying broadened areas of nursing responsibility through their definitions of nursing practice. Chapter 1 enumerates nursing functions requiring specialized judgments based on a knowledge of the physical, biologic, and social sciences. It is this knowledge base and the skill exercised in its implementation that will be interpreted by the courts when a legal problem arises and the need for a nurse witness is identified.

When a nurse is called as a witness by a court, it will be in one of two capacities: (1) as a witness to the facts underlying the controversy at hand, or (2) as an expert witness to give opinions and to draw inferences from the facts presented. These roles are vastly different, both in the nature of the testimony expected and in the preliminary preparation for testimony.

THE NURSE AS WITNESS TO FACTS

In order to distinguish these roles, it is necessary to look briefly at general courtroom procedures. Most trials constitute a reconstruction of an event or a series of events. These events are reconstructed through the use of evidence presented in the courtroom, and this evidence consists of many things. Often, the nurses' notes and other material from the patient's chart will contain highly important entries. If, for example, the notes are considered relevant to the case at hand, the nurse who made them may be asked by the court to verify the handwriting and to give the circumstances surrounding the making of the entry. For example, a patient on admission might tell the emergency room nurse that he did not know why, but he just was not paying attention when he walked in front of the bus. The nurse would make a note of this on the chart because of the possible medical significance of the comment. Later, if the patient sued the bus company for damages, the testimony of the nurse and the chart could well be used as evidence by the defendant bus company.

In addition to documents used as evidence, many other objects that are relevant to the facts may be introduced. For example, objects taken from a patient, from drugs to weapons, could become the subject of a nurse's testimony if it became necessary to identify them. Thus, when nurses are called as witnesses to the facts, they are likely to be asked to report on what they saw, were directly told, or had overheard. Observations on assessment, physical or mental, may be significant. They must speak from direct knowledge, giving facts and only facts. They are normally not permitted to tell what someone else told them, for such testimony would be considered as hearsay and would not be admissible as evidence. For example, a nurse would not be permitted to say that Patient A told her that Patient B in the next bed had acted depressed all day and carried on an argument with himself, although it may have had bearing on the fact that, later, Patient B sprang out of bed and knocked a visitor down.

In summary, professional nurses will not infrequently find themselves in positions where they are witnesses to events and to incidents that become of importance in a later legal proceeding, although they may not be the ones charged. The skill of accurate and objective observing will stand the nurse in good stead.

THE EXPERT WITNESS

Sometimes, facts alone are not sufficient evidence. The jury, a body of average citizens, may be confronted with an area of controversy so technical and complex that they are not able to reach a decision until someone having established competence in a field explains in layman's language what they could not otherwise understand. This witness is known as an expert witness.

There are a number of areas in which the testimony of the expert differs from the witness reporting the facts. The expert is given greater freedom to render opinions, but first his qualifications and expertise must be established with the court. To support these qualifications, the expert must demonstrate that his education, experience, positions held, memberships in technical or professional organizations, continuing training, scholarly writings, and awards or other recognition justify reliance on his opinions, even though he may have no direct knowledge of the specific matters at hand.

Once established as an expert, his testimony will be presented. Since he has no direct knowledge of the facts, his testimony may be presented through hypothetical questions. An example (simplified) would be: "Assume that a road was straight, dry, and with an asphalt surface. Assume further that a 5,000-pound car failed to navigate a turn, left the road after leaving skid marks 110 feet long, and that the driver had braked as hard as possible. What is your opinion as to the speed of the vehicle?''

The use of expert witnesses is not universal courtroom procedure. However, in today's complex and technologic society, many issues involving scientific, technical, and professional matters are being presented to the courts. Juries simply cannot evaluate the situation from a layman's knowledge of the field and come to a just and fair conclusion. Suppose, for instance, a pharmacist tells a customer that two drugs are identically the same in their ingredients. One costs half as much as the recognized name-brand drug. The customer buys the cheaper drug and later claims that harm resulted from the substitute drug. The distinction between the two drugs, their chemical makeup, and the physiologic consequences of their use is a matter only for expert opinion from one qualified in biochemistry or pharmacology.

THE NURSE AS AN EXPERT WITNESS

Who should the expert be, and how should he be chosen? In matters involving the standards of a profession or trade, the courts have said that the standards should be those established by members of the group under consideration. In the health fields, the general rule of law is that the expert should be chosen from the same profession as the one under scrutiny. This has been a long-accepted practice followed in the medical field. Medical malpractice, that is, the noncompliance of the physician's conduct with the standards of the community of practitioners to which he belongs, cannot usually be subject to lay opinion alone; physicians must testify before a physician can be held liable. The reasoning behind this legal rule is that the subject matter involved, namely, the standard of medical practice, is so specialized that only experts in the field can determine a departure from that standard.

There is every reason to believe that the courts would extend the same ruling to nurses. Given the professionalism of modern-day nursing, the proper expert is the professional nurse rather than any other member of the health care team. Before the nurse could be held responsible for malpractice, there should be expert professional nurse testimony showing why the nurse did, or did not, depart from an applicable standard of care. In the case of *Hiatt v. Groce*,[13] a professional nurse was charged with negligence for failure to alert the physician that the birth of Mrs. Hiatt's second child was imminent, resulting in a precipitous delivery, lacerations, and permanent damage. In his instructions, the judge advised the jury of the role of the expert.

> In determining whether a registered nurse used the learning, skill and conduct required of her, you are not permitted to arbitrarily set a standard of your own or determine this question from your personal knowledge. On questions of nursing expertise concerning the standard of care of a nurse, only those qualified as experts are permitted to testify. The standard of care is established by members of the same profession in the same or similar communities under like circumstances.

A related question is whether the physician is also qualified as an expert to render an opinion on the standard of nursing care. As nursing science is more clearly delineated as a separate body of knowledge and as nursing skills that require a scientific base for implementation become more complex, the physician will undoubtedly be reluctant to assume expertise in judging the quality of nursing care. His contact with the patient is brief; his concerns deal mainly with the therapeutic intervention for which he is responsible. He thinks, acts, and draws his opinions from a knowledge of medical science. He has little opportunity to observe the nurse giving care or to explore the body of knowledge from which nursing judgments were drawn. In fact, it is no longer logical to think of the physician as being prepared to testify on the scope and quality of professional nursing care.

Although it seems logical to think that the physician and the professional nurse might both testify as expert witnesses in areas in which they share expertise, one legal writer disagrees with this point of view:

> Allowing a physician to testify in nursing malpractice actions or a nurse to testify in medical malpractice actions simply because they share common areas of knowledge unnecessarily confuses the issue. While either might be able to explain the action to the jury, liability is based on compliance with standards of practice of fellow professionals. Thus, a nurse is being judged in comparison to other nurses, not physicians. Allowing individuals from other professions to testify tends to divert attention from evaluating the professional by compliance with his own professional standards. This distinction becomes critically important when a question of nursing judg-

ment is being evaluated. Since liability is established by reference to what constitutes competent nursing behavior, physician testimony is irrelevant. The physician can testify as to what a physician would do in the same situation, but that is not the question. The question is what a nurse should have done.[14]

THE EXPERT WITNESS AND FUTURE NURSING PRACTICE

In the health field, as well as other fields where technical and professional competence is involved, much reliance is necessarily placed on expert testimony; in such cases, it is at the forefront of the judicial process. There is every reason to expect that this situation will become ever more applicable to nursing and that, in the future, nursing experts will become more common and their testimony will become more significant.

It may be that many nurses reading this page will not be called upon to serve as expert witnesses in the legal sense. Yet, in recognizing that the final step in the nursing process is evaluation, every nurse is called upon daily to assume, to some extent, the role of an expert witness. As nurses, their colleagues, and the public become more cognizant of the extent to which professional nurses are recognized as experts in their field, the autonomous role of the professional nurse in the health care system will become more readily identified and accepted.

In the following hypothetical situation, the focus is on the skills the nurse must have to assess the condition of a patient: skills that are expected of any prudent practitioner of professional nursing. In reviewing this hypothetical case, put yourself in the place of the expert witness. Consider both the knowledge base necessary to support the proper nursing judgment and the nursing skills needed to provide an acceptable standard of care.

The expert nurse witness evaluates nursing care

FACTS. Jonathan Sprig, age 55, walked into the emergency room at Middleton Hospital, complaining of abdominal pain. Mr. Sprig was known to the emergency room staff from previous admissions, all related to his chronic alcoholism. The nurse, Frank Crane, took Mr. Sprig's vital signs and asked him to lie down on the examining table. At that time, he noted the odor of alcohol on the patient's breath and recorded that Sprig "seemed to be somewhat incoherent, as if he had been drinking." He then left the examining room and called Sprig's doctor to report his findings.

When he returned 20 minutes later, he found that the patient had either gotten up or fallen from the table and was sprawled across a chair next to the table. With the help of an orderly, Nurse Crane got the patient back on the table and rechecked his pulse and blood pressure. His blood pressure had fallen from 120/90 to 100/70, and his pulse rate, which had been 100 on admission, was now 120. Finding that Mr. Sprig was now completely disoriented as to time and place, Nurse Crane directed the orderly to stay in the room until the doctor arrived.

Forty minutes later, the doctor arrived and found the patient diaphoretic, disoriented, and vomiting copious amounts of blood. He was immediately transferred to the intensive care unit, where a diagnosis of bleeding esophagastric varices was made. He died 7 hours later.

The family brought a suit against the nurse, Frank Crane, charging that he had failed to properly assess the patient's condition and that his failure to take appropriate action contributed substantially to Mr. Sprig's death. At issue was the standard of conduct that could be expected of a professional nurse acting under similar circumstances, and the resolution by a lay jury required expert testimony.

The registered nurse, John Wright, M.S.N., who was called as the expert witness, did not have firsthand knowledge of the care the patient had received. He was given background information relative to the staffing and case load in the emergency room in which the care had been given: a staff of one supervisor, two staff nurses, one technician and an orderly. The average admissions for the service were from 15 to 25 per shift.

Mr. Wright's qualifications as an expert witness included formal training as a nurse clinician, and 5 years' experience in emergency room nursing. He was at the time the nursing supervisor of a 20-bed trauma unit in a 500-bed general hospital. He was told that, in order to support his testimony as an expert witness, he should expect to be examined on his preparation and experience, his familiarity with the current Nurse Practice Act, particularly the statutory definition for practice, the Rules and Regulations of the Board of Nurse Examiners, the Standards for Practice of the American Nurses' Association, and the opinions of nursing authorities attesting to the knowledge necessary for patient assessment and nursing intervention.

EXPERT NURSE TESTIMONY. The central issue of John Wright's testimony was whether the nursing conduct of the defendant nurse had been proper given the set of circumstances with which he had been confronted. In making his evaluation of Mr. Crane's actions, Mr. Wright would determine data necessary to arrive at a reasonable assessment of the patient's condition and the knowledge base from which nursing judgments and actions should have flowed.

In the opinion of this nursing expert, the first duty to Mr. Sprig was to adequately assess his status on admission. Considering the objective and subjective signs and symptoms presented by the patient at this time, John Wright outlined the nursing actions he would consider acceptable in carrying out the admission assessment for this patient:

1. The patient's mental acuity should have been evaluated, his perception of the pain he was experiencing explored, and the circumstances that brought it about or aggravated it considered. The extent to which the patient could relate to his present environment should have been determined.

2. Vital signs (temperature, pulse, respirations, and blood pressure) should have been taken, and heart and lung sounds should have been listened to to detect any abnormalities.

3. Observations should have been made concerning his color, skin condition (cold, dry, warm, moist), muscular coordination, and the effect of any physical exertion on cardiac and respiratory function.

4. Since the single subjective symptom offered by the patient was abdominal pain, the abdominal area should have been inspected, and its contour and the character of bowel sounds noted. An attempt to elicit further information concerning nausea, vomiting, and elimination should have been made.

5. A staff person should have been summoned to stay with the patient while telephone contact was made with the physician. At this point, in addition to reporting his findings to the physician, the professional nurse, in Mr. Wright's opinion, should have reviewed the patient's recent clinic records. With this data base, the nurse could have adequately estimated the severity of the problem and its probable etiology and whether the patient was in imminent danger.

The admission nurse, according to Mr. Wright, might well have suspected that the odor of alcohol on the breath indicated that Mr. Sprig's incoherence resulted from acute alcohol intoxication. However, drawing a conclusion from this single variable at an early stage of assessment deterred further search for additional findings. The patient might be bleeding internally, causing loss of blood volume and oxygen to brain cells. This blood loss, plus the patient's response to pain, could also be significant contributing factors to an incoherent state.

Knowledge of the patient's history of chronic alcoholism should have suggested to a professional nurse the possibility of internal bleeding from cirrhosis of the liver, with increased pressure in the portal circulation. Consequently, the nurse's plan of action should have been based on continued professional surveillance in order to detect early signs of a worsening condition because of an inadequate blood supply to vital centers.

In the judgment of John Wright, leaving the patient unattended while the doctor was being contacted violated acceptable nursing practice. The obvious deterioration of the patient, as evidenced by the drop in blood pressure, increased pulse rate, increased disorientation, and decreased coordination over a 20-minute period was strongly suggestive of either a depletion in blood volume from concealed bleeding or a marked decrease in cardiac function. Since either of these factors could result in diminished blood supply to the brain and other vital organs, the situation called for continued professional nursing assessment and a plan for intervention should the patient's condition worsen.

Furthermore, according to Mr. Wright, a professional nurse would have been well advised to place an orderly at the patient's side to prevent him from falling from the examining table if a nurse could not be in continual attendance. However, the nurse is obligated to frequently monitor changes in the patient's vital signs, mental status, physical appearance, and functioning, and to intervene if the patient continues to deteriorate. In the event that a marked change had occurred before the physician arrived on the scene, Mr. Wright concluded that, in his opinion, it would have been within the scope of professional nursing practice to order an electrocardiogram and routine blood work and urinalysis, and to administer oxygen until a more comprehensive assessment could have been made. Furthermore, the patient should have been positioned in such a manner as to maximize the flow of blood to the brain without impinging on cardiac or respiratory function. If, faced with a deepening of the shock state, the nurse elected to administer intravenous fluids, extreme caution would have been necessary. Such intervention could further aggravate the existing problem by raising the blood pressure to the point where it might increase bleeding or further tax an exhausted heart muscle, should either of these conditions exist.

ANALYSIS. Although you might not agree with all of John Wright's opinions, it is quite obvious that the scope and depth of Frank Crane's assessment and his subsequent casual surveillance of Mr. Sprig did not reflect an acceptable standard of care. The fact that he left the patient unattended and later in the care of an orderly and that he did not seek the counsel of either his supervisor or professional colleagues supports the contention that he failed to foresee the potential for harm in spite of the evidence, which pointed to a rapidly deteriorating patient for whom he was responsible. One can safely conclude that he lacked, or failed to apply, the knowledge base necessary for the practice of professional nursing in either assessment or intervention.

As all professional nurses become more aware that they are responsible for the judgments they make and that they can be held legally accountable for their actions or failure to act, cases of this tragic nature are surely less likely to occur.

8

Employer-employee liability for negligent patient care

Although there is a beginning thrust toward self-employed practice for professional nurses, it is likely that in the foreseeable future the need for a coordinated approach to health care will require the majority of nurses, along with other health care professionals, to practice within the framework of some type of health care agency.

To better understand the legal position of the nurse in this setting, it is necessary to turn away from nursing for a time and focus on a different part of the legal landscape. In this chapter, then, the concern will be not only with the conduct of the individual, but with the legal responsibility of the institution, hospital, clinic, home care program, or any other of the growing number of health care agencies by whom nurses may be employed in the course of their professional practice.

VICARIOUS LIABILITY

In one sense it is difficult to speak of the legal responsibilities of an institution. Whether it be a corporation, a nonprofit corporation, or some other legal entity, the institution itself and its directions and conduct are made up of the acts of numerous individuals. It has no life of its own; it is an abstraction, a legal fiction. To impose financial responsibility on such an entity, for whatever reason, must be justified on some basis other than the institution's own conduct for the simple reason that no one has ever *seen* a corporation or a trust nor learned how to evaluate their behavior. Therefore, in order to fix legal responsibility, the concept of vicarious liability—holding the employer responsible for the acts of its employees—has emerged. Vicarious liability is based on a relationship between parties in which an institution, person, or persons can be held liable for the acts of another and may be called on to respond legally, irrespective of actual participation in the omission or commission of the act.

Vicarious liability does not exist because the institution itself has engaged in any negligence or wrongdoing, but because, as an employer, it is subject to the legal principle that employers who receive the benefit of the acts of their employees are also responsible for the burdens that may accompany those acts. Thus a negligent error made in a hospital or in an industrial health facility may legally involve the employer because the employer could be one of those held responsible for any adverse financial consequences of such errors.

It is critical to note, however, and it must always be remembered, that this principle of vicarious liability does not relieve individual employees of responsibility for their own acts. It is an *expansion* of liability to include the employer and not a *shift* of liability away from the employee to the employer. Professional nurses who have felt secure in the belief that the liability of the employer for their conduct absolved them from legal responsibility must recognize the fallacy of their reasoning. All we have learned about the legal responsibilities of the individual engaged in nursing practice remains strictly and consistently true. Nurses must respond legally for any adverse results in their delivery of health care. The principle of vicarious liability merely provides that another person or corporate body is also responsible for the acts of the nurse.

DIRECT OR CORPORATE LIABILITY

Institutional liability may not only be vicarious, that is, liability for the misconduct of its employees, but it may also flow directly from managerial responsibility. In any health care setting, the institution owes duties to patients above and beyond the duties owed to patients by employees who give care. These duties consist of general administrative matters that the individual employee—nurse, physician, or other—may influence but not control. They are obligations that the institution itself, at its highest managerial levels, is held to have a legal responsibility to recognize and manage. For example, a hospital or other health care agency is obligated to maintain an adequate system of medical records and to ensure the safekeeping and confidentiality of all such records.

One of the expectations of those who seek the services of a health care facility is that they will receive safe, competent care. Therefore one of the principal duties of such a facility is to hire personnel whose qualifications are commensurate in education and skills to the functions they will be required to carry out. Moreover, the institution must recognize that in the present age of specialization, qualified personnel are not always interchangeable. All licensed nurses, for example, are not necessarily equal in their ability to handle a given nursing situation; a well-qualified practitioner in one area might be quite inept in another. A nurse highly skilled in the care of the newborn cannot be expected to function at the same level on an adult neurologic unit. If nurses are pressured to assume responsibility for which they are not adequately prepared and harm follows, both the institution and the nurses could be found at fault.

In the event that misassignments are made or people are hired or retained who are demonstrably incompetent, the institution will be liable for its own failure to assess employees and the needs of the positions they fill. In short, the health care facility that does not exercise due care in its employment practices puts its clients at risk and places itself in a legally vulnerable position.

Closely allied to employment practices is the obligation to maintain inter- and intradepartmental communications that ensure safe passage for the patient. While the harm that follows a breakdown in communications is generally the result of employee negligence and the cause of vicarious liability, harm resulting from failure to establish proper communication channels might find the institution itself at fault.

Another challenge to the institution is one of creating a climate for the intellectual growth of its employees. Opportunities for the interchange of ideas among colleagues, workshops, seminars, and adequate library services, are essential to maintain quality care and to prevent litigation. But when does this obligation become a legal duty? The answer probably lies in the degree to which the failure to provide such programs could be related to harm to a patient or group of patients. For example, when new and complex equipment, procedures, or treatment regimens are introduced, the duty owed the patient requires the staff be properly informed and/or instructed in order to incorporate changes in the plan of care. Failure to adequately prepare the staff to cope with new and changing situations could lead to institutional liability.

Also high in importance is the obligation to provide satisfactory equipment to carry out the services offered. If a problem arises and the institution has been derelict in fulfilling this requirement, the agency, not the employee, might be the one found at fault. If, for example, harm resulted because supplies and equipment were unavailable or improperly maintained, the hospital could be held liable because it did not provide the tools for the personnel to do their job. Similarly, institutional liability might follow the use of outmoded equipment that endangered patient safety. This problem is difficult to evaluate legally for there is no legal principle obligating every institution to maintain all types of sophisticated medical equipment. Problems of this nature are best resolved through community planning, which provides for the sharing of responsibilities and resources in the best interest of the public's health, safety, and economy. Nonetheless, a health care agency is legally obligated to provide adequate physical facilities to do the job it undertakes.

Yet another obligation, both controversial and relatively new, flows from an Illinois Supreme Court decision[15] redefining and expanding the corporate duty of the hospital and the duty of nurses as hospital employees. In this instance the hospital was held liable for failure to recognize its responsibility to oversee the quality of care given a patient by a staff physician. In addition, the nurses, who were aware of the deteriorating condition of the patient, were found negligent for failure to communicate the mounting problem to the hospital administration.

The court contended that the hospital breached its corporate duty by failing to provide the standard of care it purported to offer. The court did not follow the pattern of establishing a standard of care only on the basis of current practice in the community. Instead, it accepted as evidence the hospital's bylaws, the state statutes governing licensure of hospitals, and the Standards for Hospital Accreditation of the Joint Commission on Accreditation to which the hospital had committed itself in the accrediting process.

Had the institution been mindful of the legal significance of its stated purpose, it would have moved more positively to establish channels of communication to deal with a physician's neglect of patients. If this corporate responsibility were made known to professional personnel, channels of communication could be mutually agreed on; thus appropriate, immediate action could be taken as soon as it became apparent that the medical regimen was not providing adequate support and the patient's condition was worsening.

Obviously, the decision by hospital employees, usually nurses and doctors, to challenge the competency of any physician is fraught with the potential for great conflict. The law, however, is beginning to be quite clear in recognizing that the hospital itself has a duty independent of the treating physician to ensure that adequate medical care is provided. Professional rivalry, peer relationships, or political pressure should not stand in the way once a judgment that a physician is providing inadequate care has been made and management sees the direction of its duty.

It is important for nurses and their professional colleagues to appreciate that it is largely through the exercise of their knowledge and skills that the institution's corporate duty to provide care is carried out. Therefore professionals have an obligation to not only perform to the best of their ability but to become familiar with any documents through which the purpose of the institution is stated or that would establish valid criteria by which its actions may be judged. Such concern on the part of professional employees could go far in minimizing risk and maximizing service to those who seek health care.

LIABILITY FOR STUDENT CONDUCT IN A CLINICAL SETTING

An uncertain area in the law is vicarious responsibility of institutions and agencies for the actions of nursing and other health care students engaged in clinical learning experiences. A student who harms a patient by overreaching or breaching a duty is always responsible. Who else, if anyone, is also responsible—the instructor, the hospital, the academic institution?

The answer is speculative and depends largely on the facts and circumstances prevailing in any individual situation. It seems, however, that in the absence of payment, students would not be classified as anyone's employees. Providing the tasks given did not exceed the students' ability to handle them, neither the instructor, nor the institution, nor the school would be liable in the event that they failed to carry out the assigned tasks in a proper manner. If, however, an instructor knowingly or carelessly gave a task clearly beyond the capabilities of the student, the individual instructor might well be guilty of professional negligence if the patient came to harm. For example, a student who has not been instructed in the care of a patient with chronic obstructive pulmonary disease should not be given the responsibility of managing that patient's nursing regimen. Similarly, if a hospital knowingly permitted students to perform tasks that should be performed only by licensed and experienced nurses, it might be guilty of a breach of the duty to provide competent personnel. If corporate liability extends the responsibility of the hospital to oversee the quality of care given by a staff physician, might it not also extend to nursing care provided by faculty and students who are not employees of the institution? Once again, all is dependent on the facts of the unique situation, and generalizations are virtually meaningless.

THE DISTANCE BETWEEN EMPLOYER AND EMPLOYEE—A RISK FACTOR IN PATIENT CARE

As health care facilities expand in size and services, the gap between nurse employees and administration widens. Indeed, it may widen to the point where it threatens to endanger the very persons both are committed to serve—the patients.

As you study the incidents that follow, identify the legal principles that apply. Beyond this, visualize the structure within which the incidents evolved. Consider the responsibility of professional nursing in acting in conjunction with administration to make the work setting one in which safe care can be efficiently and effectively carried out.

"Do the best you can" nursing

FACTS. John Carpenter graduated 5 years ago from a baccalaureate nursing program. He worked for 2 years in surgery as a scrub nurse and since then has been a staff and relief evening charge nurse in the Recovery Room of Westwood Hospital. Shortly after he arrived at work one Monday afternoon, he was told by his supervisor, Olga Miller, that it would be necessary for him to assume the charge duties in the coronary care unit, a 6-bed unit staffed by two professional nurses and one practical nurse. Miss Miller explained that one of the professional nurses had become ill and had to be taken home, and the other was a new graduate in the process of being oriented to the unit.

John protested. He had not worked in a coronary care unit since he was a student, and he was totally unfamiliar with the Westwood unit. He seriously questioned whether he had the expertise to function as charge nurse there and quite frankly told Miss Miller so. She listened and said she understood his reluctance, but there was no one better qualified to fill the assignment.

Again John protested, this time pointing out that the idea of staffing a coronary care unit with two nurses inexperienced in that area of nursing was unreasonable. Miss Miller reminded him of his professional duty and said he had no choice except to "do the best you can."

As John paused to reflect on the situation, he wondered what his choices were and what the implications might be if he acquiesced or if he refused. He asked himself some questions: (1) If he went to the unit and a patient came to harm because of his lack of expertise, could he be found negligent in the legal sense? (2) Would Westwood Hospital be legally liable for his conduct if a patient came to harm? (3) What legal liability is attached to a nurse who is pressured to accept an assignment for which he believes he is not qualified? (4) What might be the consequences if he refused? (5) Was he free legally to make that decision or as an employee was he obligated to take the assignment? (6) Does the fact that he had made clear to the supervisor that he felt he was not qualified clear him of legal liability?

John found himself in the difficult position of deciding whether he should accept responsibilities that he was not sure he could meet. Even if he "did his best," it did not follow that the necessary quality of care would be given. John could see the potential for harm to the patients but, at the same time, questioned the likelihood of its occurring. He wondered if he was being overly cautious. He was accustomed to assessing a situation prior to making a decision. He thought first of his knowledge base and admitted to a good working knowledge of the pathophysiology commonly seen in coronary care patients. But he also knew that most cardiac patients are prone to anxiety and need a relaxed confident nurse, which he would not be. Next he considered the skills he would need if he took the assignment. He was familiar with cardiac drugs and the monitoring equipment currently used at Westwood. He felt he could cope effectively with a cardiac arrest, but he was unsure of his ability to assess the coronary patient and take the proper action to prevent arrest. Emergency situations were certainly not foreign to him, but he questioned whether any nurse could, in an emergency, adequately direct a team unknown to him and in unfamiliar surroundings.

ANALYSIS. The answer to some of John's questions should at this point be obvious to the reader. If John accepts the assignment, however reluctantly, he is liable for his conduct if the patient comes to harm. Through vicarious liability, Westwood would share in John's liability. Furthermore, since an institution has a corporate duty to provide competent personnel, Westwood could be directly liable for the harm.

Does John have a legal duty to accept the assignment? The answer to this question is less clear. Westwood has a duty to all it patients, but does John have a duty to the patients in the coronary care unit, since he was employed to work in a significantly different area? Since he has knowledge and skills transferable to a coronary care setting, would his duty be greater than those of a nurse who lacked these skills? What about the fact, if true, that of all those nurses available he was the most qualified?

If harm comes to a coronary care patient while John is in charge of the unit, could negligence be attached to Miss Miller since she delegated the responsibility and was aware of his perceived inadequacy? Perhaps so. The fact that she responded to John's protest by saying "do the best you can" indicates a limited understanding of an acceptable standard of care or of the legal duty owed a patient by the institution. What seems to be totally lacking from this situation is the use of the problem-solving approach. Had the supervisor, Miss Miller, recognized the sensitive legal implications of the situation, it is likely that she and John Carpenter could have worked out a plan to provide safe care. An inventory of the nursing and medical personnel might have elicited resource persons John could have called on in the event of an emergency. Thus it is apparent that the problem of transfer of employees within an institution offering a variety of services to high-risk patients is not one to be taken lightly from either a medical or a legal point of view.

A failure that threatened patients' lives

FACTS. A number of years ago a poliomyelitis epidemic swept the community of Stratford City. Anne Hobbs joined the staff of Holbrook General Hospital, where she was assigned to an adult poliomyelitis unit. After a period of orientation, she became the permanent night nurse for Ward 4F. Here she assumed responsibility for the care of six tracheotomized respirator patients, three with chest respirators and three with tanks.

At 5 o'clock one morning, she was in the utility room next to the ward preparing equipment for morning care when she heard a pounding noise coming from the ward. She investigated immediately and found the patient next to the door, who was in a chest respirator and fortunately had some use of his arms, pounding feebly on his bedside unit.

A quick survey of the scene told Anne that the three patients in chest respirators were not being ventilated—no chest movements were apparent. To the right, the three tank respirators were operating. Aware that the three patients had only minimal function of their respiratory muscles, Anne knew that time was a critical factor. Quickly she reasoned that only a power failure would take out three respirators at once, but why were the respirators to the right functioning?

Anne's first impulse was to call for help, but considering the time factor she chose not to. Instead, she pushed one bed across the room and connected it to an outlet; the patient's chest began to rise and fall. Quickly she did the same for the other two beds. Now all the respirators were working. Only then did Anne take time to look at the three patients and to see fear slowly fading from their faces.

When the ward was settled, the patients cared for and calmed, and the respirators checked, Anne took time to call the night supervisor to report the incident. Imagine her frustration to hear, "Oh, didn't someone call you? There is a power failure downtown, and we've gone to our emergency equipment. I guess it doesn't service the whole house!"

ANALYSIS. Fortunately, no harm came to the three respirator-dependent patients, but if harm had come to them, who would have been at fault? Suppose that, acting in haste, Anne had not accurately diagnosed the problem but had used valuable minutes to call for help or confer with her nearest colleague. It is quite possible that the limited respiratory reserve of the three frightened patients would not have been sufficient to sustain life. Would Anne have been legally negligent? You can only answer by asking: what could one expect of a reasonably prudent nurse in a like situation?

If Anne were found negligent, her employer, Holbrook General Hospital, could share in her negligence. But what if Anne were not found negligent. Could Holbrook General be held directly liable for the harm that came to patients as a result of failure to provide communication that would have warned Anne of the impending danger? Was the institution negligent in not providing sufficient staffing to allow for increased nursing coverage for such totally dependent patients? Perhaps, but what of nursing's responsibility to work in concert with administration to foresee and prevent such disasters?

Summary

The fact that in both of the foregoing incidents the supervisor appeared at fault is not a reflection on the general ability of those who hold supervisory positions. It does, however, point to the problem of distance between top-level management and the staff nurse. This distance is far too wide to be bridged by one person with the multiple duties usually assigned to the position of supervisor. Until those at the management level and the care givers move to reduce this distance, problems will mount and the patient will be lost in an avalanche of directives and distorted communication channels.

Section three

RIGHTS OF PATIENTS IN HEALTH CARE FACILITIES

The history of modern nursing reflects the profession's continuing commitment to patient-centered care. This commitment is illustrated in the introductory hypothetical situation in which the nurse, Patricia Guise, demonstrated that the patient's rights were central to the plan of care.

In her initial assessment of Mrs. Yancey, Patricia saw an alert, cooperative patient not unduly concerned with her illness but obviously determined to remain in control. Consequently, she was not surprised when Mrs. Yancey flatly refused to have a nasogastric tube passed until she was seen by Dr. Roman. As she reassessed her patient's condition an hour after admission, Patricia could not help but be concerned. In that hour, Mrs. Yancey had deteriorated considerably and Patricia seriously doubted that she was capable of making a rational decision relative to her treatment.

Patricia had always firmly believed in the right of a patient to participate in his care and that therapy must not be initiated without the patient's informed consent. Now she was called on to judge whether or not this patient had the capability to participate in an important decision regarding her care. She was convinced that the nasogastric tube would provide relief of symptoms. Yet to pass the tube against the patient's wishes might not only be physiologically and psychologically harmful to the patient but could even be judged an unlawful invasion of individual rights, deliberate tortious conduct.

Patricia's dilemma is not an uncommon one and involves an

element of risk, since she must not only decide whether or not the patient is mentally competent to make a decision but also must determine whether or not the proposed action will make a significant difference in her recovery.

Obviously, the resolution of such a problem rests on the judgment of the nurse, but the following chapters, devoted to the legal exploration of the rights of patients, should offer positive guidance helpful to nurses who must make decisions where the rights of patients are in question.

9

The basic human right to be
free of intrusion

In our crowded and complex society, each of us is buffeted from all sides by constant reminders that our rights are limited by, or may often be in conflict with, the rights of others. We are frustrated by the simple physical crowding of our daily lives. We may not even be aware of the fact that the law provides us with significant individual protections, in the sense that it will provide us with a remedy in the event that certain of our rights are needlessly impinged upon.

The term *intrusion* as it is used in this chapter is a very broad one and should not be thought of as being limited only to bodily harm. It may include psychologic harm caused by another; it may include the stress induced by threat of physical action; it may include restrictions on one's freedom of movement; or it may include the invasion of one's privacy. In all of these senses, freedom from intrusion is a right honored by the law and one that can be expected to receive the protection of the courts.

MEANING AND SCOPE OF RIGHTS

A *right* is a capacity or a privilege, the enjoyment of which is secured to the person by law. The law has identified certain rules for the control of human conduct, which are quite apart from injury-producing situations. These rules flow from *rights* or *interests* that hold for all persons and may not be violated without incurring legal liability, unless the individual consents to their invasion.

It is interesting to note that the first ten amendments to the Constitution of the United States, adopted in 1791, deal with human rights. Among these are the right of freedom of speech, the right of protection from un-reasonable search and seizure, the right to a speedy trial, and the right to due process of the law before being denied life, liberty, or property. It is doubtful that our democratic form of government would have endured without these safeguards.

Nurses throughout the world have long had concern for the rights and responsibilities that they felt should be exercised in the care of patients. The International Congress of Nurses in 1953 developed a *code of ethics,* which was revised in 1965 and again in 1973. In all of these documents the subject of rights was viewed in an ethical rather than a legal sense.

Following the pattern set by the International Congress of Nurses, the American Nurses' Association in 1950 adopted a *Code for Nurses.* Although the underlying legal implications of this code are significant, they are not identified as such. The code was and is intended to guide the individual nurse in the practice of nursing consistent with ethical principles.

Consider, however, the legal potential in selected items from the ANA *Code for Nurses* as it was revised in 1976:

1. The nurse provides service with respect for human dignity and the uniqueness of the client unrestricted by considerations of social or economic status, personal attributes, or the nature of health problems.
2. The nurse safeguards the client's right to privacy by judiciously protecting information of a confidential nature.
3. The nurse acts to safeguard the client and the public when health care and safety are affected by the incompetent, unethical, or illegal practice of any person.
4. The nurse assumes responsibility and accountability for individual nursing judgments and actions.
5. The nurse maintains competence in nursing.
6. The nurse exercises informed judgment and uses individual competence and qualifications as criteria in seeking consultation, accepting responsibilities, and the delegating nursing activities to others.
7. The nurse participates in activities that contribute to the ongoing development of the profession's body of knowledge.[1]

Thus the profession has identified issues dealing with ethical nursing conduct. At the same time it has publicly recognized that the recipients of health care have certain basic human rights that must not be intruded on by those who provide the service.

Presently, as part of the total concern for the rights of individuals, the rights of patients have been receiving increasing attention on national, state, and local levels. Of considerable importance is the statement known as *A Patient's Bill of Rights,* which was issued by the American Hospital Association in 1973. Sweeping in scope, it has been the subject of intensive medical and legal scrutiny. This document focuses on the challenge to community based health organizations, including hospitals, to define and protect the rights of patients who utilize their institutions. Some of the rights that have been identified in the statement are:

1. The patient has the right to considerate and respectful care.
2. The patient has the right to obtain from his physician complete current information concerning his diagnosis, treatment, and prognosis in terms the patient can be reasonably expected to understand. When it is not medically advisable to give such information to the patient, the information should be made available to an appropriate person in his behalf. He has the right to know by name, the physician responsible for coordinating his care.
3. The patient has a right to receive from his physician information necessary to give informed consent prior to the start of any procedure and/or treatment. Except in emergencies, such information for informed consent should include but not necessarily be limited to the specific procedure and/or treatment, the medically significant risks involved, and the probable duration of incapacitation. Where medically significant alternatives for care or treatment exist, or when the patient requests information concerning medical alternatives, the patient has the right to such information. The patient also has the right to know the name of the person responsible for the procedures and/or treatment.
4. The patient has the right to refuse treatment to the extent permitted by law, and to be informed of the medical consequence of his action.
5. The patient has the right to every consideration of his privacy concerning his own medical care program. Case discussions, consultation, examinations, and treatment are confidential and should be conducted discretely. Those not directly involved in his care must have the permission of the patient to be present.
6. The patient has the right to expect that all communications and records pertaining to his care should be treated as confidential.
7. The patient has the right to expect that within its capacity a hospital must make reasonable response to the request of a patient for services.
8. The patient has the right to be advised if the hospital proposes to en-

gage in or perform human experimentation affecting his case or treatment. The patient has a right to refuse to participate in such research projects.

■ ■ ■

No catalog of rights can guarantee for the patient the kind of treatment he has a right to expect. A hospital has many functions to perform, including the prevention and treatment of disease, the education of both health professionals and patients, and the conduct of clinical research. All these activities must be conducted with an overriding concern for the patient, and above all, the recognition of his dignity as a human being. Success in achieving this recognition assures success in the defense of the rights of the patient.[2]

Some critics of the *Patient's Bill of Rights* have questioned its ambiguity. For example, what is meant by current and complete information concerning a diagnosis? Moreover, does the right of a patient to obtain information concerning his illness imply that nurses, or other health professionals, have the obligation to act when it appears that a physician has not fully disclosed information concerning his diagnosis and/or prognosis to the patient? In reference to the patient's right to privacy, the statement prohibits persons not directly involved in the patient's care from participating in case discussions unless permission to be present is granted by the patient. What constitutes direct involvement? Does this standard limit case discussions as a tool to be used in the preparation and continuing education of health care personnel?

Undoubtedly, the *Patient's Bill of Rights* places a burden on the hospital. The right to refuse treatment is clear if such refusal is not in violation of the law. The right to considerate and respectful treatment waves a legal flag that could trigger a suit. Although the *Patient's Bill of Rights* does not have the force of law, it could be persuasive in court proceedings arising from breakdowns in patient care. Furthermore, it undoubtedly influences many health care agencies in the formation and adoption of policies, which, upon adoption, they are generally obliged to enforce.

Another indication that the public is becoming more aware of the rights of patients is the growing demand for an authorized patient representative within the health care setting. Increasing numbers of health care facilities, either voluntarily or in response to legislation, have created the position of patient advocate or ombudsman. The patient advocate gives the patient another way to be heard and assists in finding answers to troublesome questions. The outlet thus provided the patient may serve as a preventive measure in avoiding litigation.

Important as this position is, and it will probably become more so, it does not relieve nurses or other health professionals from recognizing and dealing with the rights of patients. It must be appreciated that the rights of patients are not incidental to the conduct of health care personnel but are at the very heart of any decision making or action taken in the delivery of health care. Therefore all health practitioners are patient advocates.

INTENTIONAL INTRUSION ON ANOTHER'S RIGHTS

There are basically two ways in which a person's rights may be intruded on: the negligent or inadvertent act and the deliberate or intentional intrusion sometimes referred to as the intentional tort. We have discussed in preceding chapters the yardsticks for measurement of negligent conduct; our concern now is to consider standards by which intentional intrusion will be measured.

Certain criminal activities—assault, battery, murder, armed robbery, a simple mugging—all involve an intentional intrusion on a person by another. But what is meant by intentional? The robber with gun in hand who takes another's purse is doing what he consciously desires and intends. But what of the jokester who playfully points a gun and shoots intending to miss but instead wounds? This too is intentional conduct. "For conduct to be intentional, there must be *the conscious performance of an act, either for the purpose of accomplishing a particular result or where a reasonable man would believe that a particular consequence of the act would be very likely to occur.*"[3]

Perhaps paramount among rights is the right each of us is granted to be free from imposition of physical harm, however slight, by agencies under the control of other persons. Stated in another way, this means that if our physical person is intruded on by others, or by anything under another's control, and that invasion results in damages, we are entitled to monetary compensation for that damage from the other causative agent.

Moreover, the term *physical intrusion* as it is used here has a very broad meaning and may be extended to include psychologic harm caused by another, or it may include the stress induced by threat of physical action.

In addition to the right to be free of physical harm are other related rights protected by law. One of the principal ones and one increasingly threatened by a rapidly expanding technologic society is the right to privacy. This right, in a broad sense, means seclusion from others and confidentiality of one's personal affairs. It also means holding one's self or property from personal scrutiny—a right to be left alone and to be free from unwarranted publicity.

Another right, essential and useful to a productive life, is the right of freedom. If this right is restricted, we may have the right of redress against those who restrict it. If, for example, we are confined against our will without valid reason, we may be able to institute an action against those doing it for the tort known as false imprisonment.

In all of these senses, a right is honored in the law and protected in the courts.

THE NATURE OF RIGHTS IN A HEALTH CARE SETTING

Consumerism in health care services has been slow to develop, for when people are ill, they tend to relinquish their rights, without question, to those who supposedly will make them well. On recovery they prefer not to think about any inadequacies of the health care system and consequently fail to take positive steps to protect the rights of others. Lately, however, consumer criticism and inquiry have been directed toward the rising costs of health care, malpractice claims, and human experimentation. As a result, attention has been drawn to the health care system and to any practices that might jeopardize individual rights.

Basic to the question of patients' rights is the fundamental principle that a patient in any health care setting retains his legal rights. He maintains his right to be free of physical harm; he maintains his right of privacy; and he maintains his right to be unrestricted in his movements. Indeed, the status of the health care patient does not result in the forfeiture of any legal rights. And, as in any other case, if these rights are infringed upon, legal remedies may ensue.

Nearly all forms of health care—and nursing in particular—invade the right to be free of intrusion. From the extreme example of the surgical removal of limbs or organs to the milder intrusions involved in simple personal care of the body, the patient's person is in fact subjected to continuing invasion. Imagine the degree of invasion involved in the removal of an arm if this were done in a setting other than the operating room. This somewhat dramatic illustration should cause nurses to reflect on the apprehension with which patients, especially those who are inadequately prepared, react to procedures. Consider the reaction of a patient when a nurse, armed with a tray of unfamiliar equipment, announces without explanation that she is about to carry out a task that, although therapeutic, physically intrudes on the person of the patient.

The right of privacy has long been recognized in relation to confidentiality of communications and in freedom from publicity. Recently the legal scope of the right of privacy has been broadened to include a recognition of human beings' spiritual natures, feelings, and intellect. Gradually, this right has come to mean the right to enjoy life, which includes the right to refuse lifesaving therapy and even the right to die.

Consider the degree to which the right of privacy is sacrificed by a hospital patient whose room is open at any time, virtually on an unrestricted basis, to hospital employees whom the patient does not know. Doubtless he would object violently if such persons were to exercise comparable privileges in his home. Far too often the right of privacy is forgotten under the urgency of providing care in emergency situations or under circumstances when the needs of the institution or its personnel take precedence over those of the patient. Instances of intrusion on the right of privacy range from unnecessary exposure during a physical examination to the dissemination of personal information to those not involved in the care of the patient.

Similarly, the right of freedom is clearly one that can be easily violated in a health care setting. Some restrictions on freedom may well be necessary, either for the effective administration of the hospital or for the safety of the patient. Restraints are well known and, at times, necessary implements of health care but it must be emphasized that they do restrict freedom and therefore intrude on the rights of the patient. The invasion of this right, like others, may be consented to, and this is the only basis for confinement in a health care setting. Thus it is essential that health care practitioners recognize that their day-to-day activities hinge on a series of important rights and that these rights may be invaded only on the basis of consent.

NURSING'S RESPONSIBILITY FOR OBSERVING PATIENTS' RIGHTS

Consideration of the integrity of the rights of patients is only as secure as the commitment of those who have the authority to protect them; this responsibility rests chiefly with the nurse and the physician. Their subtle recognition of the rights of patients can permeate the climate in which health care is delivered. It is largely their responsibility to see that any invasion of individual rights is not justified solely in the name of teaching or research. In most instances, the patient can consent to and become an informed and interested party in these activities. Teachers and researchers should recognize that by safeguarding the legal rights of patients they augment and strengthen patient care and the learning process.

Little has been done by nurses to examine those activities that are distinctly nursing and require the nurse to make a judgment as to whether an action infringes on the rights of the patient or whether it is a justifiable interference with those rights. This kind of self-study, along with collaboration with other members of the health team in examining the entire patient experience, offers a challenge to deliver health care that is sensitive to both the needs and the rights of the patient.

It is now a legal mandate that the physician can no longer be the sole determiner of the need for treatment or for surgical intervention. We shall see in the chapter to follow how the patient and his family may become active participants in planning for therapeutic intervention. How should nurses react if, in their opinion, an uninformed patient has made an unwise decision about his health or even his life? Disclosure on which an informed consent may be based is no longer the sole prerogative of the physician. As the care plan evolves, the nurse must accept with the physician a joint responsibility for evaluating the degree of the patient's understanding and knowledge so that the patient, in turn, can exercise his right to give or withhold consent.

THE RIGHTS OF THE MENTALLY ILL OR INCOMPETENT

Nurses who care for persons judged to be mentally handicapped, regardless of etiology, must guard diligently against any violation of their basic human rights. Their concern for the safety of the disabled person or of others close to the person cannot allow the patient's right to dignity, privacy, or freedom to be infringed upon without careful study of all possible alternatives.

Working from a data base established by an assessment of the patient and his environment, a plan must be constructed that allows the individual the right to have the least restrictive or invasive conditions necessary to achieve the goals set for his continuing care or recovery. In this area of nursing the responsibility of the professional nurse for judging behavior and foreseeing potential harm looms large. However, if nurses recognize that the mentally ill have legal rights, and if they can explain the rationale for any intervention that may seem to violate these rights, they can feel reasonably secure that their conduct will not be legally challenged, or, if challenged, that it can be defended.

For example, a significant assessment factor in relation to the Standard of Psychiatric Mental Health Nursing Practice which relates to psychotherapeutic intervention reads:

> Limits are set on behavior that is destructive to self or others with the ultimate goal of assisting clients to develop their own internal controls and more constructive ways of dealing with feelings.[4]

Thus the nurse who determines the need to restrain, isolate, or by some other means curb a patient's behavior must be able to justify this action in terms of the positive effect it is expected to produce in the resocialization or safety of the patient or those around him.

NURSING DUTY VERSUS PATIENTS' RIGHTS

The patient is first a person. This fact is often forgotten in the concern of the health team to initiate a plan of care based solely on medical considerations. All too often those considerations, while seemingly significant, are not understood or accepted by the person most concerned, the patient. Disclosure may have been overlooked, or decisions may have been the exclusive prerogative of the physician, the nurse, or the health team. Regardless of the process, the patient is on the outside looking in at the phenomenon of self under the control of others, and even if those others are well-meaning and competent, the experience is disturbing and degrading.

In the situations that follow, examine the duty as seen by the nurse and rights as viewed by the patient. Where did they take divergent paths? Could the resulting conflict have been prevented? Have rights been violated and, if so, do you believe the nurse was aware of the nature of the right intruded on?

A patient's refusal leads to intentional intrusion

FACTS. Maude Wilson, a middle-aged woman with rheumatoid arthritis, has been under the care of Dr. Bart for a number of years. She is an intelligent woman, understands her illness, and has, for the most part, accepted without question any therapy that has been prescribed.

Maude is well known to the nursing staff at Prescott General Hospital. She has always been a cheerful and cooperative patient, seeming, in spite of her limitations, to enjoy life. However, during her last admission for correction of chronic anemia associated with her arthritic condition, she has seemed discouraged with her failure to respond to treatment. She is easily fatigued, complains of constant pain, and spends much of her time in bed with the door to her room closed and the shades drawn.

As part of his treatment regimen, Dr. Bart prescribed an iron dextran injection (Imferon), one injection daily for 3 days, to be followed by further laboratory assessment. On the morning of the third day the head nurse, Vicki Powers, was visiting Maude when the team leader, Alice Perkins, brought in the medication. Maude looked at Alice and said angrily, "If that's that shot, I won't have it. It isn't helping and its making my hips so sore I can't move."

Vicki reached across the bed and gently rolled Maude toward her saying quietly, "Now Maude, this will be the last one for awhile so let's get it over with." Quickly and with skill, Alice injected the drug. In a burst of anger Maude raised herself up on one elbow and glaring at Vicki shouted, "Get out of my room." Then she lay down, closed her eyes, and refused to respond to either Vicki or Alice.

Later that day Mr. Wilson approached Vicki at the nurses' station. Calmly and with dignity he informed her of his displeasure with the treatment of his wife and made it plain that it was his intention not to let the matter drop.

ANALYSIS. Situations similar to the Wilson incident are not uncommon. Nurses acting in response to their knowledge of the health needs of patients are often prone to consider that a patient's refusal of treatment lacks validity, and consequently their perception of duty runs counter to the patient's perception of his right.

It is almost certain that neither Vicki Powers nor Alice Perkins felt that the administration of Imferon against the expressed wishes of Mrs. Wilson constituted a violation of her right to be free of intrusion. Their actions undoubtedly were based on their desire to carry out a regimen that they expected would be beneficial to the patient. However, if a charge of battery were brought, could it be supported?

When Maude Wilson entered Prescott General Hospital, she did not surrender her legal rights; therefore she had, like any other person, the right to be free of physical intrusion. Could the injection of a drug prescribed by a physician and properly prepared and administered be the agent of physical harm? The answer to this must be considered in relation to certain facts. First, the conduct of the nurses in this instance was intentional, for it was the conscious performance of an act for the purpose of accomplishing a particular result—the administration of a drug. Second, Mrs. Wilson refused the injection and her refusal was ignored. Third, the right to be free of physical harm encompasses the right to be free of emotionally or intellectually offensive conduct. For Mrs. Wilson the deliberate injection of a drug without her consent might well have been seen as intellectually and/or emotionally offensive conduct and an intentional intrusion on her right to be free of physical harm. The facts do not argue well for Ms. Powers and Ms. Perkins.

Since the *Patient's Bill of Rights* and the *Code for Nurses* have been offered as guidelines for protecting patients' rights and ensuring quality care, the nurses' conduct may be measured in terms of those guidelines.

1. Were they cognizant of the patient's right to refuse treatment?
2. Was their disregard of Mrs. Wilson's refusal of the medication indicative of a lack of respect for the human dignity and uniqueness of their patient and a violation of her right to considerate and respectful care?
3. In their failure to recognize the significance of the behavioral change in their patient and in their haste to carry out a procedure against the wishes of the patient, did they demonstrate a degree of incompetence not compatible with professional nursing practice?

Perhaps the simplest explanation of the conduct of Ms. Powers and Ms. Perkins is that they acted on their knowledge of what they knew was accepted therapy for Mrs. Wilson's condition. The conduct is explained, but is it justified?

Learning threatens to invade privacy

FACTS. Under the leadership of their head nurse and with the approval of nursing service, the nursing staff on Seven South had initiated the practice of weekly case discussions during which they engaged in in-depth study of one patient. The patient selected was usually one who presented a challenge to the staff, and the end result of the discussions was definite professional growth and increased job satisfaction.

Marge Coffman, R.N., chose for her presentation Harriet Brown, who had undergone surgery for the treatment of ulcerative colitis. Harriet had presented a number of problems, physical and emotional, to the staff during the 4 weeks she had been on the unit. She was particularly close to Marge, who had taken on the responsibility of teaching her how to care for and live with her ileostomy. During the relationship, she had revealed to Marge a good deal about her unhappy childhood, her ambivalent feelings about her parents, the difficulty she had had in adjusting to her marriage, and now her fear of rejection by her husband.

Marge was well prepared for her case presentation. Her main objective was to help the staff understand the nature of the illness and the need for supporting the patient through the crisis associated with radical surgery and preparing her for reentry into the community. The conference was held on the sun porch, which also served as a lounge for patients and visitors, and ran beyond the allotted 40 minutes. In her haste to get back to the unit, Marge left the notes she had prepared on a window ledge.

Several hours later the cleaning woman, noticing the patient's name and room number on the cover page, assumed that the notes belonged to Mrs. Brown and took them to her. When Mr. Brown arrived for his evening visit with his wife, he found her in tears. He examined the notes and immediately called nursing service demanding an explanation of why his wife's privacy had been invaded, threatening to sue the hospital and insisting that his wife be transferred to another unit immediately.

ANALYSIS. Clearly Harriet Brown has been subjected to a traumatic experience, but has her privacy been violated in the legal sense? Does the nursing staff have the right to discuss the illness and treatment response of a particular patient without the consent of the patient? According to the guidelines set down in the *Patient's Bill of Rights,* consent is necessary only for persons not directly involved in the patient's care. Since all those present at the conference had been at one time involved in Mrs. Brown's care, that standard was met. However, was the right of the patient to expect that all communications pertaining to her care be kept confidential violated by Marge Coffman? The fact that the notes prepared by Marge were available for several hours to anyone entering the sun porch could be the basis for arguing that Mrs. Brown's personal life was opened to public scrutiny, and therefore her right of privacy was violated.

Without resolving the question of whether or not Mrs. Brown's right of privacy had been violated in the legal sense, it can be assumed that failure to safeguard her privacy was far reaching in its consequences. During a critical stage in her recovery, it caused her to lose confidence in those she had come to trust. It quite possibly strained the relationship between herself and her husband, and it forced her to reorient herself to another hospital unit and another nursing staff at a time when trust in others was at its lowest. All of these consequences suggest that Mrs. Brown had been subjected to psychologic harm. Perhaps the health profession's richest resource for learning is the study of the patients they serve, but the right to utilize that resource can only be justified if the privacy of the patient can at all times be assured.

Patient conformity and restraint of freedom

FACTS. James Abernathy is a distinguished appearing gentleman in his late seventies. Since his wife died 5 years ago, he has lived alone, although he is visited frequently by his daughter, Frances Hobbs, a legal secretary. Mr. Abernathy takes a good deal of pride in being independent. He manages his affairs well and, although a somewhat reserved person, has continued to be involved in community activities through membership in several civic organizations.

During his last annual physical examination the doctor palpated a mass in the abdomen and recommended hospitalization for a gastrointestinal workup. Mr. Abernathy entered the hospital at 4:00 P.M. That evening a laxative was given in preparation for a barium enema on the following day. At 10:00 P.M. the nurse advised Mr. Abernathy, who was sitting in a chair reading, that is was time to retire. He thought not, explaining that he was a night person and rarely was in bed before 1:00 A.M. About 20 minutes later the nurse returned with a sleeping pill, again advising Mr. Abernathy that he better get some sleep as he would "have a busy day tomorrow." The medication was taken but not without some hesitation and protest by the patient who argued that he never took sleeping pills and that he would not need one if he were allowed to follow his usual routine.

One hour later Mr. Abernathy awakened. Apparently confused by the strange environment and the depressive effect of the sedative drug, he stumbled into the hall and fell. He was discovered immediately by the nursing staff, lifted back into bed, and examined for injury. Because he seemed confused, restraints were applied and the side rails raised. During the process of getting Mr. Abernathy into bed the signal cord was disconnected, leaving him without ready means of communication.

At 7:00 A.M. Ms. Hobbs stopped at the hospital on her way to work and found her father restrained in a bed soiled with feces and urine. He was still somewhat groggy but oriented and greatly chagrined to find that he had been restrained. He related what he thought had happened, demanded to be taken home, saying that he "would rather die than be drugged and tied in bed." His daughter acquiesced but not without warning the nursing staff that she intended to initiate a grievance against those responsible for his care.

ANALYSIS. It seems quite obvious that the point at which the nurse and Mr. Abernathy disagreed as to what was a reasonable hour for him to retire was the moment at which the patient's rights and the nurse's duty came into conflict. We can safely assume that the conduct of the nurse was well intentioned. It is probably true that she was more aware of the difficulties Mr. Abernathy would face on the following day than he was. Was it reasonable, however, for her to assume that inducing an unnatural sleep at an earlier hour than the patient was accustomed to retiring would necessarily lessen the problem? Should she not have been aware that a sedative drug administered to any patient, and particularly an elderly person, often provokes a confused restless state rather than a normal sleep? Should she not have considered that the need to make decisions for oneself is basic to all persons and often becomes even more valued as a person advances in years and perceives his decision-making ability to be eroding? Was she sufficiently aware of Mr. Abernathy as a person, or was his individuality submerged in the need to carry out a prescribed regimen?

Why did Mr. Abernathy submit to the nurse's wishes? Probably because, like many others, he is subconsciously indoctrinated with the idea that in entering the hospital one surrenders his right to make decisions for himself. Furthermore, the conduct of the nurse reinforced this feeling. Had she been committed to the idea that the patient should be involved in decisions regarding his care, the sedative drug might not have been administered and the patient's confused state might not have followed.

Although it is difficult to assess in the abstract whether or not restraints were necessary to protect the patient, it cannot be denied that they were applied without the patient's consent and of a certainty restricted his freedom. Should not other measures, less violating to basic human rights, have been tried? If the protection of the patient was of primary concern, why was the disconnected signal cord overlooked? Nursing can ill afford to wait for a challenge by the courts to be stimulated to more constructive approaches for safeguarding the welfare of confused patients.

Ms. Hobbs' decision to institute a grievance may well result in better care for future Mr. Abernathys. She is aware that, under existing statutory law, a mechanism to deal with patient grievances has been instituted. Under this procedure, it will be necessary for her to submit the grievance to the hospital's patient advocate. If the grievance cannot be resolved at this level, the complaint is referred to the chief executive officer of the hospital for further investigation of the circumstances surrounding the incident; he will then report his findings to the complainant. If the complainant is still dissatisfied, the problem is referred to the Executive Director of the State Health Department who, in turn, investigates the incident and reports his findings and recommendations to the hospital and to the complainant.[5]

The outcome of such proceedings can do little to restore Mr. Abernathy's dignity or to compensate for the intrusion on his right of freedom. What it can do is bring into proper perspective the rights of patients and the obligation of the health care system to seek better methods of providing care without impinging on those rights.

When nursing knowledge was not enough to protect a patient's right

FACTS. Three weeks after his twenty-ninth birthday, Joe Fisher underwent colostomy surgery for cancer of the sigmoid colon. It was a difficult period for Joe, but he was determined that life was not over for him. He was convinced he had a problem that he alone had to deal with. When the time came for him to be instructed in colostomy care, he rejected the idea of involving his wife, saying he would take that step later.

With the capable help of Phyllis Carlson, R.N., who had cared for him throughout the postoperative period, he made rapid progress. On the morning he was scheduled to carry out the irrigation procedure for the first time unassisted, with Phyllis standing by to help only if necessary, a disturbing event occured.

As he was about to begin the procedure, the head nurse called Phyllis to the nurses' station. The director of nursing had telephoned to say she was sending three nurses, who were assigned to the hospital as part of a "refresher course" and who needed experience with colostomy patients, to observe Mr. Fisher's irrigation and stoma care.

Phyllis, knowing how Joe guarded his privacy, suggested that the observation should not be allowed. The head nurse accepted Phyllis' opinion and told her to call nursing service and explain the circumstances. Phyllis hesitated, then went back to Joe's room and told him some nurses would be coming in to observe. They came. They observed a procedure in which everything went wrong. Joe was tense, Phyllis equally so. Owing to the inadequacy of the morning irrigation, it was necessary to change Joe's dressings several times during afternoon visiting hours. Joe appeared withdrawn and discouraged.

The next day Joe asked his doctor to discharge him. The doctor did but only after planning for follow-up care in the home by a public health nurse.

ANALYSIS. Phyllis Carlson brought Joe Fisher to the point of independence through a carefully thought out and executed plan of care. To that point she had been functioning at a professional level. Insightful in her assessment of Joe, she had kept him informed of the treatment regimen and involved him in decision making. Suddenly she failed and in her failure violated her patient's right of privacy.

Phyllis realized that, given the choice, Joe would have refused permission to be observed. The harm that flowed from her conduct was evidenced in the failure of the irrigation procedure and in the patient's subsequent behavior.

Since Joe pressed no charge that his rights were violated, the question of legal liability is not pertinent to this analysis. What is pertinent is why Phyllis acted as she did. She had the nursing knowledge necessary to make the right decision. What was lacking? What further knowledge would have caused her to act on her convictions?

Had Phyllis really understood her patient's right to privacy, her conduct might have been different. Knowing that she could be held liable for contributing to the violation of his rights could have guided her to act as an autonomous person, in control of her conduct and ready to accept accountability for her actions.

Summary

Writing under the title, *Notes on Hospitals,* published in 1859, Florence Nightingale made the rather startling pronouncement that "It may seem a strange principle to enunciate as the very first requirement in a Hospital that it should do the sick no harm.''[6] True, the concerns that compelled her to make such a statement were far different from those currently expressed, yet the basic principle is as valid today as it was more than a century ago.

There are countless ways in which health care personnel go about the business of preventing harm to those who are the recipients of their service, not the least of which is developing competence in their selected area of practice. But as has been seen in the preceding hypothetical situations, competence and/or good intentions are not always sufficient to prevent harm. Is it not possible that a legal knowledge of the basic human right to be free of intrusion could be the most fundamental factor in ensuring that the health care system would do the patient no harm?

10

The meaning and mythology of consent

Every human being of adult years and sound mind has a right to determine what shall be done with his own body, . . .[7]

In the preceding chapter the rights of individuals were discussed, and it was emphasized that legal protection of those rights was not lost on one's entry into the health care system. Once a person knows his rights, how does he then choose to surrender them, and by what means does he do so in order to maintain or restore health? Although it is a complete reversal of the time-honored axiom, "the doctor knows best," it is the thinking of health care practitioners today that the patient is a participant in making any decisions involving his welfare. Patients usually want to cooperate and assist in bringing about recovery. The nurse, however, needs to know the legal means of enlisting this cooperation without violating rights of the patient to be free of intrusion. That is the thrust of this chapter.

LEGAL RELINQUISHMENT OF INDIVIDUAL RIGHTS IN A HEALTH CARE SETTING

Given the fact that the patient retains his rights and that the medical and nursing profession continually invade those rights, how can such invasions be legally justified? Why is it than an arm can be amputated without the surgeon having to respond to damages? It is tempting to answer this question by saying the patient has benefited, that it is good for the patient, or that he is better off with the invasion than without it. While these answers may be true in a general sense, they are not legally valid. They imply a value judgment made by a person other than the patient, a judgment as to what is good for the patient.

The fact is that under the law the only person who can make such a judgment is the patient himself. If the patient makes the judgment that he is better off with a certain procedure being performed, then he gives his *consent* to that procedure. This consent frees the person performing the procedure from legal responsibility for intrusion on the patient's rights. The person is free of legal responsibility not because the patient is better off or may be better off, but because he has given his consent. Without that consent, no amount of perceived well-being to a patient can justify an intrusion on his individual rights. The fundamental underlying principle is that each person has the right to determine how and under what circumstances he will receive health care. The right to consent implies the right to refuse, and that right too is recognized in the law as is illustrated in the following case.

In *Goedecke v. Department of Institutions,*[8] Goedecke underwent a court-requested psychiatric examination and was diagnosed as a paranoid schizophrenic. The examining psychiatrist determined that he was dangerous and gravely disabled. The specific basis for the "dangerous" finding was based on Goedecke's arrest for assault and for his verbal threats against a judge and others. He was ordered to be detained for short-term treatment in a mental institution, to be followed by continuing outpatient treatment.

A behavior modification drug was ordered. The patient objected to taking the drug, for he had taken it previously and had experienced the unfavorable side effects of falling down, loss of breath, stiffness of the tongue, and disordered thinking. In spite of his objection, the drug was administered even though a statement of objection signed by Goedecke was filed in the chart. Later, medical testimony corroborated the short-term side effects of the drug, and stated that long-term use often produced a neurologic condition known as tardive dyskinesia, depression, and suicidal behavior. Furthermore, "Milieu therapy (a beneficial environment with a positive attitude on the part of the staff and an opportunity to participate in physical therapy and occupational therapy)" was available as a desirable alternative in treating paranoid schizophrenia.

The issue was whether a patient should be submitted to therapy without his consent and over his objection. The court ruled that a person being treated for a mental illness has the right to privacy and dignity as well as the right to refuse treatment, and that voluntary rather than coercive measures should be followed.

DISCLOSURE AS THE BASIS FOR CONSENT

Disclosure is a process not limited to the delivery of health care. Within a broader context, it simply means the release of information or the giving of knowledge in order to achieve a certain purpose. In health care, however, it means the conveyance of information by which a patient acknowledges the need to relinquish certain rights in order to bring about a desired therapeutic result. The need for adequate disclosure is not limited to acts performed by physicians; disclosure must be the initial step and a continuing process in the implementation of any significant phase of patient care by any health professional.

In order for consent for health care to be valid, it is essential that the patient be fully advised of all possible consequences, that all relevant facts be disclosed to him, and that he understands how these facts and consequences relate to him as a person. Only with such knowledge and understanding can consent be given. Without knowledge of relevant facts and the mental capacity to provide consent, any consent granted will be ineffective. It follows then that if a patient has not validly consented to the intrusion on his rights and intrusion takes place, those responsible for it may be held legally liable for the intrusion. A consent form signed under the influence of drugs or after inadequate disclosure will not be recognized by law. Consent must be genuine, not a matter of obtaining a signature or a verbal assent regardless of the circumstances under which it was obtained.

It is particularly important to recognize that the process of disclosure brings to the patient an understanding of what his consent means and that this understanding is a prerequisite for valid consent. In this process the physician, under our laws, owes the patient the duty of full disclosure of diagnosis and of possible consequences of any course of treatment in order for the patient, if he so desires, to give his informed consent. One can imagine many medical regimens wherein possible side effects or long-range problems might not, in the patient's mind, justify their utilization. Whether or not the cure is worse than the disease is entirely up to the patient, and it is up to the physician to see that the patient understands.

It is a narrow view of disclosure to assume the physician is the only one whose duty it is to inform the patient. Good professional nursing care has always called for disclosure as a prelude to consent to any and all steps in the implementation of care. For example, nursing has long recommended that the reason for a treatment, the need for a particular position in bed, or the effect of a drug should be shared with the patient. As modern nursing widens its horizons to accommodate functions such as diagnosing and treating human responses to actual or potential health problems, the nurse's legal responsibility in the area of disclosure and consent becomes more significant.

DISCLOSURE ALLOWS FOR PATIENT INVOLVEMENT

Knowledgeable, clearly worded disclosure, then, is the pivotal point on which consent rests. Too little attention has been given to this legal requirement as a positive component in patient care. Failure to disclose has been sounded as an evil force bringing charges of malpractice. A more positive and reasonable approach to the subject of disclosure is to view it as the right of the patient to have access to information that pertains to his life and well-being.

As professional nurses teach or communicate with patients, they are continually disclosing information on which they will base care. For example, the professional nurse who recognizes disclosure as the root of care will not only assess the condition of a surgical patient but will, to the extent possible, involve him in the postoperative regimen. Explaining to the patient why some blood clots might appear in a drainage tube and advising him to call the nurse if the tube fails to clear lessens anxiety and provides the patient with the incentive to participate in his care.

When a patient questions any part of a therapeutic program, nothing can so compound his anxiety and loss of confidence in nurses as to have them say, "You will have to talk to your doctor." Such a response not only frustrates the patient but also threatens the ego of the nurse who, in making the statement, denies the intellectual ability to function in the situation.

In general, the health care professional who initiates a plan of care or who is responsible for its execution is the one who should disclose significant information to the patient. He is the one who is likely to be held legally accountable for obtaining the patient's consent to his plan of therapy. This may be a physician, a nurse, a social worker, or any other health professional. A simple rule to follow in determining what and when to disclose is to consider what the patient has a right to know and what he needs to know in order to cooperate or to refuse care. An informed patient is usually a cooperative patient with a reasonable chance to obtain optimum health, and that is what health care is all about.

LIMITATIONS ON DISCLOSURE

Disclosure is fraught with many variables. In each instance there is an element of judgment based on facts, and there is the question of how to disclose with minimum risk of an untoward reaction on the part of the patient.

In interprofessional relationships no one member should fill the gaps in disclosure for another without consultation with that person. For example, in talking with a patient, the nurse sensed that he was not alert to possible risks of the contemplated therapy. The nurse discussed the situation with the physician and learned that he had consciously elected not to fully disclose certain adverse factors. In the discussion, it was decided that the physician would talk with a member of the family whom the nurse knew to be receptive and able to deal with the situation. Thus, through consultation within the health team, disclosure was accomplished and the well-being of the patient was safeguarded.

Many malpractice charges have focused on failure to disclose. This has led some health professionals, who are overly concerned with legally protecting themselves, to disclose prematurely at the expense of the patient. The primary care nurse who advised the patient with impaired hearing that he would be likely to experience "real trouble in a few years as the otosclerotic changes in the middle ear progress" undoubtedly created undue anxiety on the part of the patient. Although probably correct in this assessment, such an approach to disclosure was ill-timed, because of its negative outlook on a condition that might have been treatable, or, if not wholly curable, slow in becoming a serious problem.

Another common error in disclosure is minimizing risks in order to secure consent. Heavy assurance can amount to a guarantee of cure when, in fact, the outcome is more likely to be amelioration rather than cure. The nurse who, in a preoperative discussion, tells a frightened patient that a gastric resection "will take care of all your stomach problems" is exercising more deception than disclosure. The relationship of the nurse to the patient is a fiduciary one, meaning a relationship of confidence, trust, and good faith. If a patient is unable or unready to accept full disclosure, the fiduciary relationship places a greater burden on the nurse. There are no easy answers to the problem of disclosure, but honesty and concern for the patient must prevail.

CREATING AN ENVIRONMENT FOR INFORMED CONSENT

As scientific knowledge expands, health care services must grow to accommodate new resources and technologies. The health care recipient often experiences a feeling of being lost in the system. Compounding this problem is the fact that expansion of knowledge results in specialization and more fragmentation of care. Under these circumstances great care must be taken to minimize the deterioration of personal relationships. Impersonal care creates a climate of bewilderment and dissatisfaction for health care receivers and legal vulnerability for the care givers.

If the patient does not understand what is being done, why it is being done, or by whom it is being done, his reaction may be passive or non-confronting. Such behavior should not be mistaken for consent. Nonresistance is not equal to consent. Consent is a voluntary act and requires the exercise of sufficient mentality to make an intelligent choice to do something proposed by another.

Thus a patient must have sufficient knowledge of the nature of the transaction—be it surgery, nursing care, or some other form of therapy. He also needs to know the person or persons who will be accountable for the transaction before he can give informed consent. It is here that a coordinated team effort is imperative. There is little room in the health care system for competition and power plays among the professionals. The right of the patient at all times supersedes the right of any one profession or professional.

In the absence of an emergency, the patient must be given the option of living with illness or accepting treatment and assuming its risks. Although a valid consent to treatment requires disclosure of risks, it need not go to the extreme of including such possibilities as an improperly performed procedure or an unlikely drug reaction. The right of the person to be informed must not be confused with a recitation of remote hazards that would only alarm to the point of refusal and so interfere with the patient's chance for recovery.

It is equally important for the patient to know that in giving consent he has not for all time relinquished his right of refusal. A valid consent can vanish should the giver choose to revoke it. The health team must recognize the potential right of the patient to refuse or revoke his consent and should be prepared to acknowledge this in discussing alternate courses of action.

WHO GIVES CONSENT

When a patient in a health care facility is able to understand procedures, absorb facts, and make a valid judgment, only that patient may make a judgment as to what should be done with his body; consequently he is the only one who can consent to an invasion of his rights. If the patient is unable to do so or, as in the case of children, is unable to comprehend and make a valid judgment, a family member or legal guardian must be advised and consulted. In a situation in which a patient is temporarily unable to give consent and the circumstances do not call for immediate treatment, the action should be delayed until the patient can make a judgment about the course of treatment.

It should be noted that parents do not have unlimited freedom to refuse treatment on behalf of their children. In the event that judgments made by parents for children are life-threatening or deprive a child of optimum health, the courts will not permit the child's rights to be lost. There are a number of legal decisions where the courts have intervened and authorized treatment after parents have refused to give consent for reasons that were sincere to them or based on firm religious convictions.

THE USE AND MISUSE OF CONSENT FORMS

An unsafe approach to the process of obtaining consent is to have a consent form signed by the patient as a routine part of the hospital admission procedure. This form purports to consent to virtually anything that anybody on the health team feels is a necessary part of care. If a patient questions signing over such broad powers, he may be told by the admission clerk, "You must sign or we cannot admit you to the hospital." This consent would fail to meet legal requirements on several counts: First, a blanket consent without disclosure is invalid. Second, consent obtained by coercion is no consent at all. Third, the health care practitioners who give patient care are the ones legally accountable for securing the consent.

In the pressure of processing the admission, little effort is made to help the patient understand the extent to which he is authorizing the invasion of his rights by others. The saving part of this process for the patient is that a blanket consent is virtually useless as a shield or device to free a physician or nurse from the responsibility for full and honest disclosure.

Closely related to the blanket consent is the consent form often signed immediately before surgery at the request of a staff nurse. The artificiality of such a procedure is obvious. Under these circumstances the patient is usually consenting without adequate disclosure by the one legally responsible for securing the consent, the surgeon. It is apparent that neither the blanket consent nor the routine surgical consent are panaceas for the consent problem since they do not meet the criteria for informed consent. Once again, the touchstones for a valid consent are a knowledge of the procedure and its consequences and the capability to give consent based on that knowledge. Anything short of that, no matter how memorialized by paperwork, will not be regarded by the courts as a legally valid consent.

This is not to suggest that consent forms cannot be made legally sound. The wording of the form must, however, verify the fact that the patient understands the procedure to which he has consented and that he has had the opportunity to raise questions and to know that he, the patient, is the one to weigh the alternatives and make the decision. Generally speaking, it is the manner in which the form is used as well as the form itself that provides the basis for consent.

VERBAL CONSENT

The more structured form of consent is the written form, which, to be valid, must be accompanied by sufficient interaction between the patient and the health care giver to permit the patient to understand what he is signing and why he is being asked to give his consent. With the professional nurse, as with other professionals, verbal consent is the more usual way for the patient to allow for the invasion of his protected interests. In order to receive necessary care he may verbally consent to physical intrusion, invasion of his privacy, restriction of his freedom, or any combination thereof. The principles of disclosure and consent apply with the same legal force to verbal consent as they do to the written method. The person providing the care is obliged to see that these principles are not violated.

How does the nurse's conduct give tacit recognition to the patient's rights in carrying out day-to-day nursing activities? A long time ago, nurses may have taken a step ahead of other professionals in discussing their plan of action with patients. For example, through disclosing the reasons for holding the patient to a certain limitation of fluids or in reassuring the patient that intravenous fluids will help to relieve thirst, the nurse invited patient participation in his care. In fact, one cannot envisage quality nursing care that violates the principles of disclosure and consent.

There is always the possibility that after the nurse explains what should be done, the patient will refuse the treatment stating that he has suffered enough discomfort and simply wants to be left alone. Good nursing practice, sensitive to the legal implications, would require that the nurse explain the consequences of refusal in a nonthreatening way. In the end the patient is the one who makes the choice and the nurse must abide by the decision. The fact that a patient is not able to make a rational decision does not negate the need for disclosure of contemplated nursing care. It then becomes necessary for the nurse to turn to a member of the family or to the person legally responsible for the patient to obtain consent for any care or treatment that could be said to intrude on the basic human rights of the individual receiving care.

CONSENT—THE PRIORITY OF ITS POSITION
IN THE PLAN OF CARE

Nurses have long held to the premise that care is based on need and that in assessing patient needs the nurse must rank the needs in terms of the order in which they should be fulfilled. Nurses have also consistently focused on the importance of informing the patient about the nature of the care to be given and what he can expect from that care. Perhaps it is now time to put the emphasis on consent. Patient consent should follow careful assessment and disciosure and must assume priority over any action.

In the hypothetical situations that follow, it will be seen that consent was either overlooked or inadequately dealt with by the nurse. In a health care system, supposedly designed to serve the patient, why should this be?

Silence that was not consent

FACTS. Mrs. Agatha Rogers had lived most of her life in the farming community of Hillsbrook. Shortly after her fifty-ninth birthday she suffered a stroke that left her with right hemiplegia and motor aphasia. Initially, she was cared for at home by her daughter, Mrs. Doris Tyler, a nurse. However, since both her family and her physician believed she would benefit from more intensive physical and speech therapy, arrangements were made to admit her to the Rehabilitation Unit of Metropolitan Hospital, 60 miles from Hillsbrook.

Mrs. Rogers was transferred by ambulance accompanied by her 17-year-old granddaughter, Terry, who had been involved in her care since the onset of her illness. Terry remained with her grandmother until the close of evening visiting hours.

Her first night alone in a strange environment was difficult for Mrs. Rogers, for she was acutely aware of her inability to communicate effectively with the staff. Terry returned to the hospital in the morning to help her grandmother with her breakfast. After breakfast Hilda Vance, R.N., entered the room, introduced herself, and proceeded to explain that the doctor had ordered an indwelling catheter since Mrs. Rogers was incontinent during the night. She immediately set about preparing the patient for the procedure. Although she explained in some detail what she was doing and why, she failed to notice the distressed look on her patient's face or that Mrs. Rogers was moving her left hand in a protesting gesture.

Three days later Mrs. Tyler visited her mother. She was surprised and dismayed to find that it had been necessary to insert an indwelling catheter since her mother had not been incontinent since the first week of her illness. After talking with Terry, she was convinced that her mother had tried to communicate disapproval.

Mrs. Tyler confronted the nursing staff, charging that they had carried out the procedure without an authorized consent. She contended that the catheter was not necessary and that her mother's incontinence was a result of failure on the part of the staff to establish communication with an aphasic patient. The doctor was consulted, the catheter was removed, and together Mrs. Tyler and the nursing staff worked out a more suitable plan of care for the patient.

ANALYSIS. Like many patients whose illness has resulted in a temporary or permanent neurologic deficit, Mrs. Rogers needed a champion. Obviously, the patient's right to be free of physical intrusion was not protected. It is ironic that a professional nurse, who is committed to give care that is personalized and based on individual need, should have been the one to violate that right.

It is likely that in the case of Mrs. Rogers the problem began to take shape when she was admitted to the rehabilitation unit. If this is true, Mrs. Rogers' family might to some degree share the blame for her inadequate treatment with the nursing staff. If a member of the family had discussed with the staff their experiences in caring for Mrs. Rogers or, more important, if someone on the nursing staff had taken an adequate nursing history, the problem of incontinence could have been avoided. While it is suggested that the family had a duty to Mrs. Rogers, it is far exceeded by the duty owed to the patient by the professional staff.

It is commendable that the nurse who inserted the catheter explained what she was doing and why. At the same time it must be admitted that she was communicating to, but not with, the patient. Should she not have been fully aware that a patient without speech has other ways of communicating that she must heed? In any event, Mrs. Tyler was correct in assuming that her mother's rights had been intruded on without her consent. Silence on the part of the patient does not necessarily mean consent.

When consent becomes a ritual

FACTS. Adolph Meyer, age 52, had a long history of gastric symptoms. He was an impatient man, changing physicians frequently and rarely following a recommended regimen. When he consulted Dr. Adams about his symptoms, hospitalization for diagnostic work was advised. The actual procedures to be followed were not discussed nor was Mr. Meyer encouraged to ask questions. Mr. Meyer agreed to enter the hospital only after he had been assured by Dr. Adams that he would not be in the hospital for more than 2 or 3 days.

Among the orders left by Dr. Adams was one for morphine sulfate, 10 mg, to be given on call from the gastrointestinal laboratory. The drug was administered by Louise Mason, R.N., at 10:00 A.M. Twenty minutes later Dr. Adams' office nurse called to ask the head nurse to have Mr. Meyer sign a consent before leaving the unit.

At 10:30 A.M. Ms. Mason brought the consent form to Mr. Meyer's room. Unsure herself of why a consent was being asked, she explained rather vaguely that it was hospital policy to obtain the patient's consent before certain diagnostic tests. Since, by that time, Mr. Meyer was beginning to experience the effect of the morphine, he did not question the request and, with some effort, scrawled his signature on the form.

By the time Mr. Meyer reached the laboratory he was quite oblivious to his surroundings. Communication between the patient and Dr. Adams and the laboratory staff was minimal. Unfortunately for Mr. Meyer, Dr. Adams, and Nurse Mason, the examination was not uneventful. In passing the fiber gastroscope, the esophageal wall was injured, and as a result the patient's stay in the hospital was considerably prolonged.

Mr. Meyer did not charge Dr. Adams with negligence. Rather, he based his contention on the fact that he had not been advised of the nature of the examination and its inherent risks before entering the hospital and that his consent for the procedure was obtained after he had been sedated. He was convinced that his rights had been violated and sought legal redress from Dr. Adams and the hospital.

ANALYSIS. It is quite apparent that the consent signed by Mr. Meyer was not valid. His scrawled signature supported the contention that he was under the influence of a drug when the form was signed, and there was no evidence to indicate that an effort had been made to disclose the nature of the procedure for which he was being prepared.

Dr. Adams' first error in judgment was in assuring Mr. Meyer that his hospital stay would be short. That in itself could be construed as minimizing risk to secure the patient's consent. Furthermore, he failed to communicate to either the patient or the nursing staff the diagnostic procedure he was contemplating. As the person who would perform the procedure, he was the one legally accountable for securing the patient's consent. In defense of his conduct it must be said that he did not know the drug had been administered before the patient was asked to sign the consent form.

It is possible the hospital could incur liability vicariously through the conduct of its employee, Louise Mason, since she was the one who carried out the consent ritual. Even though she was not accountable for securing the consent, she had a duty to act affirmatively when the quality of care given fell short of meeting the patient's need. There can be no rational explanation for seeking consent from a patient whose ability to think logically could be clouded by a narcotic drug. There is also no reasonable excuse for a nurse to ask a patient to consent to a procedure when neither she nor the patient knows what procedure will be carried out. Certainly professional nursing must be based on judgment, not on the exercise of rituals.

Summary

It is well established that a society cannot exist without language or some form of communication. However, there are times when language ill serves its purpose. In the situations just reviewed, one cannot help but

question why professional nurses would be guilty of conduct that so bla-
tantly violated patients' rights and good nursing practice. Perhaps the word
order may be at the root of the problem. From early childhood, we learn
that an order must be obeyed or dire consequences will follow. It is a
powerful word and one that provokes an action response.

But is it not a denial of the patient's rights to assume that a doctor can
order the nurse to invade a person's legally protected interests? Changes in
the language through which the physician communicates his proposed
treatment regimen might in time create an environment in which the right
of the patient gains primacy in the implementation of care. Let us consider
deleting the word *order* from the care plan and see if this change in language does not help consent gain priority over action.

Section four

THE NURSING PROCESS LEGALLY REVISITED

In the foregoing chapters legal authority for nursing practice has been discussed. Instances of nursing conduct have been analyzed in terms of selected legal principles. A positive correlation between quality of nursing care and legally defensible nursing conduct has been established. The ongoing integration of law into the nursing process has been offered as a logical approach to responsible nursing practice.

Another area for study of nursing accountability is the examination of legal principles used in reasoning a litigated case. As with other areas of law, the usefulness of the litigated case has not been widely recognized by the nursing profession. Over the years nurses have been exposed to only a limited view of case materials. The tendency has been to dwell on the facts of the incident and to give superficial treatment, if any, to the law on which the decision was based. Today's professional nurse, prepared in the technique of critical analysis, should be able to recognize in the legal decision the area of nursing conduct that has been evaluated, and should understand that the precedent established by a particular decision may guide the development of the law of future nursing practice.

11

Nursing conduct legally examined

While an increasing number of professional nurses choose to search primary sources and extract relevant data from legal writing and cases, others may need an additional incentive. To challenge its members to become interested in litigation, some professions, medicine among others, have given to the legal departments of their professional associations the responsibility of preparing monographs dealing in depth with current legal issues. In these monographs carefully researched pieces of litigation relative to a particular issue are assembled and discussed. When a court has taken note of social change calling for change in practice, such cases are analyzed and made available to any interested professionals.

A similar service could be of inestimable value to professional nurses. If digests of litigated cases dealing with nursing practice were made available to nursing practitioners, the relevance of law to nursing would be made clearer and more real. Upon being intellectually challenged to examine the scope of a case, nurses should perceive in the legal situation what in actuality is an account of nursing practice. They should think of the knowledge the nurse had or should have had, but did not use, in assessing and acting. They should be aware of the point at which the quality of nursing practice broke down, and should consider appropriate steps to ensure patient safety and improve the quality of nursing care.

Assuming that this service could be supplied, nurses would need some structure to facilitate the effective use of this type of material. To this end, a method of case analysis is offered for professional nurses who are interested in enlarging their perception of the law of nursing practice. The technique consists of three sequential steps in identifying why the court ruled in a given situation and the relationship of the judicial decision to the practice of nursing:

1. Examination of the *fact pattern*—what actually happened to bring the misconduct to the attention of the court
2. Identification of the *legal principles* used in the judicial decision—their relevance to recognized components of nursing care
3. *Nursing analysis*—consideration of the conduct to which the legal principles applied and of the impact of the power of precedent on future nursing practice

The third and final step is the critical part of the case review. Through it, errors in past nursing conduct are examined and the significance of precedent established by the court on future nursing conduct is weighed. The use of this method will be illustrated by examining two cases: *Delicata v. Bourlesses,*[1] and *Mirhosseiny v. Board of Supervisors of Louisiana State University.*[2] As presented, these cases are extracts from decisions of the appellate courts. The language of the published court opinions is used. The only omissions are those of legal procedure and citations of previous cases and authorities.

DELICATA V. BOURLESSES[1]

DIGEST. The plaintiff, Delicata, seeks to recover damages for the death of his wife and for the loss of consortium, as a result of alleged malpractice of the defendant, a nurse. The action was considered by a medical malpractice tribunal, which concluded that the plaintiff's offer of proof did "not present a legitimate question of liability appropriate for judicial inquiry." The action was dismissed, and the plaintiff appealed from the judgment of dismissal. The appellate court concluded there was an error in the tribunal's finding because the plaintiff's offer of proof was sufficient under required standards to raise a legitimate question of liability appropriate for judicial inquiry.

The offer of proof presented to the medical tribunal consisted of the following documents: (1) a written statement by the plaintiff; (2) a copy of the records of the New England Deaconess Hospital for the period from November 17, 1975, to November 22, 1975, when the plaintiff's wife was confined to a psychiatric ward for treatment for a depressive reaction after her first suicide attempt; (3) a copy of the patient incident report concerning the death of the plaintiff's wife; (4) the plaintiff's wife's death certificate; (5) a copy of the further answer of the hospital to one of plaintiff's interrogatories; and (6) the affidavit of Heide A. Scholten, a registered nurse, dated February 19, 1979, which expressed the opinion, based on her examination of the material in the foregoing documents, that the standard of nursing care provided by the defendant to the plaintiff's wife on the night she committed suicide deviated from good and acceptable nursing practice.

In March 1975, the deceased, Carmela Delicata, then age 39, was suffering from cancer. In March 1974, she had undergone a left mastectomy. The operation was followed in January 1975 by a right pleural effusion and oophorectomy. Sometime after her last surgery, she was informed that the cancer had metastasized in her bones, and she commenced chemotherapy. In the late summer of 1975, her overall condition caused her to become depressed. On November 15, 1975, while at home and in the presence of her daughter, she attempted suicide by placing a towel around her neck and choking herself. As a result of this incident, she was treated at the Newton-Wellesley Hospital, and on November 17, 1975, she was transferred from the facility to the psychiatric ward of the New England Deaconess Hospital. The nurses' notes in the New England Deaconess Hospital reveal that on November 18, 1975, she was "[t]ense, anxious and worried that she would have a nervous breakdown. . . . Frightened . . . . Very depressed wants to die." On November 19, 1975, she expressed a desire to commit suicide and asked the staff "to assist in the task of suicide." She was placed under constant supervision but was seen by a staff psychologist, who "advised that patient should not be under supervision constantly." The hospital records reveal that she was also examined on November 19 by a staff psychiatrist, who felt that suicidal precautions were not necessary. On November 20, 1975, she attempted to refuse her chemotherapy medication, stating she wanted to "give up" and that she felt as if she were "going crazy and losing her memory." On November 21, 1975, she was observed by the nurses to be "[a]ngry and defensive. Extremely [down]. . . . [Feels] she is not worth attention. Stating she is 'crazy' and feels it is time to go to the 'nuthouse.' Fearful and depressed. . . . Seems bewildered. . . ." On November 22, 1975, she was again examined by the staff psychiatrist, who urged that "she have ECT [electroshock therapy] beginning on November 24th. . . . [I] asked her to discuss this when her husband visited that evening. She was somewhat resistant to the idea of treatments and reassurance was not helpful." That evening, another patient overheard and related to the staff a conversation between the deceased and her husband, in which she told her husband that this was a "nuthouse" and she "wanted to die." Her husband apparently replied that he was disgusted with her and left shortly thereafter. The balance of the nurses' notes in the record for that night is as follows:

> Patient last seen at 9:00 P.M. when she went to draw up a bath. At 9:40 went in search of patient. Door to bathroom locked. Called her name twice—no answer—went to get master key to unlock door. Found patient fully clothed submerged in water filled tub. Pulled from water to half-sitting position. Patient's face was purple. Pounded on chest. No respiration, pulse or response. Upon pounding chest projectile gush of fluid from mouth. Mayday called. Attempted resuscitation without success. Patient pronounced dead 10:10 P.M. Dr. Sheldon notified—medical examiner notified.

"The progress notes of the psychologist begin with the diagnostic impression of "[d]epressive reaction (moderate)" on November 17, and end with the conclusion on November 21 that the patient was "[v]ery depressed." During her hospitalization she was confined to rooms without bath or shower facilities and, according to the plaintiff, "[f]or her to take a bath or shower she had to go out to another room specially for the purpose of taking a bath or shower." The cause of death was listed on the death certificate as "asphyxia due to drowning (while depressed). Generalized carcinomatosis secondary to mammary carcinoma." In a further answer by the hospital to the plaintiff's interrogatories, the defendant was identified as its employee assigned to the deceased's care on November 22, 1975, between 3:00 P.M. and 11:30 P.M.

Heidi A. Scholten, a qualified registered nurse with experience in psychiatric and mental health nursing, stated in a sworn affidavit that she had examined the foregoing documents and that, based on the facts contained therein and on her own educational training, knowledge and professional experience in the field of psychiatric and mental health nursing, she had the opinions: (1) that "both the nursing notes and nursing assessment report indicated that Mrs. Delicata was suicidal, severely depressed and exhibited a worsening clinical condition"; (2) that "[t]he clinical condition of Mrs. Delicata . . . warranted and required visual observations of her at least once every (15) minutes"; (3) that the defendant, in particular, because she was assigned to the patient, had the responsibility "to insure that such visual observations . . . were made"; (4) that the defendant's failure to observe the patient for a forty-minute period amounted to a "deviation from good and acceptable [n]ursing [p]ractice and [p]sychiatric and [m]ental [h]ealth [n]ursing [p]ractice"; and (5) that the defendant's conduct was a contributing cause of the death."

It was the duty of the tribunal to evaluate the evidence summarized above in a manner comparable to what a judge presiding at a civil trial would do in ruling on a defendant's motion for a directed verdict. Under this standard, the plaintiff, in order to sustain a cause of action in negligence for medical malpractice against the defendant, was obliged to establish: (1) that a nurse-patient relationship existed between the defendant and the plaintiff's wife; (2) that the defendant's conduct failed to conform to good nursing practice because the defendant failed to provide the deceased with the degree of skill and care expected of the average nurse under the circumstances; and (3) that the defendant's negligence was a contributing cause of the death.

The further answer of the hospital to the plaintiff's interrogatory that the defendant was the hospital employee assigned to the deceased's care between 3:00 P.M. and 11:30 P.M. on November 22, 1975, establishes the first element. Indeed, the defendant's brief concedes that, taken in the most favorable light, the plaintiff's offer of proof established that "there was a duty owed to the plaintiff's decedent by defendant nurse . . . to the extent that the plaintiff established that Nurse Bourlesses was assigned to the care of the plaintiff's decedent [on the night in question]." The opinions expressed in the affidavit of the plaintiff's expert, based on the facts contained in the documents she examined, were sufficient to establish the scope of the duty owed by the defendant and to warrant a finding that that duty had been breached. The plaintiff's expert indicates that the hospital records available to the nursing staff would alert a reasonably competent nurse in a similar situation that Mrs. Delicata's clinical condition was worsening throughout her stay at the hospital. The affidavit raises the inference that on the evening of November 22, 1975, the deceased had a motivation and desire to commit suicide. The deceased's adverse reaction earlier in the day to the notion of electroshock therapy, together with her comments to her husband that she wanted to die and his expression of disgust with her (both of which were brought to the attention of the staff), and her exit at 9:00 P.M. from her room into a separate bathroom for a bath, and remaining in the bathroom without a check for forty minutes, warrant a finding that the deceased had been left in a potentially dangerous situation unattended and unobserved for an unreasonably lengthy period of time. The affidavit of the plaintiff's expert also permits the conclusion that, despite the psychiatrist's finding three days before that suicidal precautions were unnecessary, a reasonably skillful nurse in the defendant's position would, at a minimum, have monitored Mrs. Delicata during the bath, based on the patient's condition that evening, or should either have instituted closer supervision on her own initiative or sought permission from a staff physician to implement stricter controls. The opinions expressed by the plaintiff's expert properly define the appropriate legal standard of care and are in keeping with the requirement that in the usual medical malpractice case the jury must be guided by expert medical opinion in order to determine whether the conduct of the medical defendant toward the patient violates the special duty which the law imposes as a consequence of a particular medical relationship.

The element of causation presents a question of fact for the jury. The assertion by the plaintiff's expert, based on her review and assessment of the medical facts in the documents, that the defendant's conduct was "a contributing cause of the death" would warrant a conclusion by a rational jury that closer supervision of the deceased by the defendant in the course of the evening and particularly during the bath might have averted the incident. There is nothing in the record to support the notion that the opinion by the plaintiff's expert as to causation is based on conjecture. "Where the relation of cause and effect between two facts has to be proved, the testimony of [a medical] expert that such relation exists or probably exists is sufficient . . . ." Finally, because the offer of proof was sufficient to show probable malpractice on the part of the defendant, the tribunal should not have excused or exonerated the defendant from responsibility on the basis of perceived negligence on the part of other medical personnel charged with the deceased's care. The question of possible negligency by other tortfeasors was not properly before the tribunal, and, in any event, a particular tortfeasor would not be relieved of liability for the entire harm she has caused just because another's negligence might also be a factor in effecting the injury. The established rule is that an injured party is permitted to sue a tortfeasor for the full amount of damages for an indivisible injury that the tortfeasor's negligence was a substantial factor in causing, even if the concurrent negligence of others contributed to the incident.

The judgment, the order for a bond and the present finding and decision of the tribunal are all vacated; that finding and decision are to be replaced by a new finding and decision to the effect that the plaintiff's offer of proof discussed in this opinion is sufficient to raise a legitimate question of liability appropriate for further judicial inquiry.

Examining a fact pattern in a litigated case

With what degree of objectivity does a professional practitioner read the account of a charge against a colleague? Often, the tendency is to overanalyze the facts or even to dispute their credibility. A reinterpretation of the evidence may be unwittingly given in an attempt to justify the conduct of the practitioner. This is a futile exercise and tends to nullify the real value in studying the case.

The facts of any litigated case are shown by the legally accepted evidence in dispute. What was the nature of the harm? What actually happened to cause the harm? Were there overriding policies or traditions that took precedence over patient needs? Did there appear to be a connection between the harm that occurred and the conduct of the person or persons accused of bringing about the harm?

In *Delicata v. Bourlesses,* the plaintiff, Donato Delicata, sought to recover damages for the death of his wife and loss of consortium as a result of the alleged malpractice of the defendant, Nurse Ann Bourlesses. To seek a causal relationship between the alleged harm and the conduct of the nurse, one must turn first to the facts. In examining the fact pattern in any litigated case, a nurse might well follow the steps used in the nursing process and begin with an assessment of the patient and his environment.

In this instance, one finds a 39-year-old woman, Carmela Delicata, admitted to the psychiatric unit of New England Deaconess Hospital on November 17, 1975, where a diagnosis of moderate depressive reaction was made by a staff psychologist. Her history disclosed that in March of 1974 she had undergone surgery for cancer of the breast. In 1975, she was told that the cancer had metastasized and chemotherapy was initiated. On November 15 of that year, she attempted suicide in the presence of her daughter. It was this act that brought about her admission to the psychiatric unit. On November 19, Mrs. Delicata asked the nursing staff to help her commit suicide. Following this incident, she was placed under constant supervision until seen by a staff psychologist, who advised against this precaution. A staff psychiatrist who saw her on the same day concurred in this opinion.

Mrs. Delicata continued to show evidence of depression—refusing chemotherapy, saying that she wanted to give up and that she was "going crazy." The nurses' notes described her as "angry and defensive," "fearful," "depressed," and "bewildered."

On November 22, Mrs. Delicata was again seen by the staff psychiatrist, who urged her to have electroshock therapy and asked her to discuss this with her husband. That evening, another patient reported to the staff that he had overheard her tell her husband that she "wanted to die." Mr.

Delicata apparently replied that he was disgusted with her and left shortly thereafter.

Mrs. Delicata was last seen at 9:00 P.M. when she went to draw a bath. At 9:40, she was found submerged in a water-filled tub. Resuscitation was attempted without success. The cause of death was listed as "asphyxia due to drowning (while depressed)."

Having looked at the fact pattern in relation to the patient, one should look more specifically at the actions taken by the nursing staff in providing care for Mrs. Delicata. The nurses' notes indicate that the nursing staff recognized early that they were dealing with a tense, frightened patient who expressed a desire to die. After Mrs. Delicata asked for assistance in taking her own life, the nursing staff placed her under constant supervision until advised by medical personnel that this precaution was not necessary. While the nursing record continued to show deepening of Mrs. Delicata's depression, with feelings of worthlessness, anger, and defensiveness, there was no evidence that the nursing staff proposed a reestablishment of the protective regimen they had once thought necessary. When she was "somewhat resistant" to the suggestion that she receive electroshock therapy, reassurance was attempted but was "not helpful." Furthermore, there is nothing in the record, as reported, that the staff took any action when a fellow patient reported the rejection of Mrs. Delicata by her husband on the evening of her death. In fact, it is clear, from the nurses' notes, that 40 minutes elapsed from the time Mrs. Delicata was last seen until someone went to check on her.

The defendant, Ann Bourlesses, was the hospital employee assigned to Mrs. Delicata's care at the time of her death on November 22, 1975.

Identifying the legal principles used in the judicial reasoning

The plaintiff, Mr. Delicata, sought to recover damages for the death of his wife because of the alleged malpractice of Ann Bourlesses. The action was considered by a malpractice tribunal, which concluded that the plaintiff's offer of proof did "not present a legitimate question of liability appropriate for judicial inquiry." Mr. Delicata appealed the judgment. The court of appeals summarized the proof offered by the plaintiff and concluded that there was an error in the tribunal's findings since the offer of proof was sufficient to raise a legitimate question of liability appropriate for judicial inquiry.

The principles of legal duty, standard of care, the duty to foresee harm, and causation are all reflected in the deliberations of the court. Since it was established that Ann Bourlesses was assigned to the care of Mrs. Delicata on the night of her death, there was clearly a legal duty owed to her by the defendant. In determining whether the evidence established that defendant's conduct conformed to an acceptable standard of nursing practice and whether it was a substantial factor in the cause of death, the court referred to the opinion of the expert witness, Heidi A. Scholten, a registered nurse with "educational training, knowledge and professional experience in the field of psychiatric and mental health nursing."

Nurse Scholten, having examined the facts, stated her opinion in a sworn affidavit. Her examination of the nurses' notes and nursing assessment report confirmed that Mrs. Delicata was suicidal, severely depressed and exhibited a worsening clinical condition. It was her judgment that Mrs. Delicata's condition necessitated visual observations at least every 15 minutes, that the defendant had the responsibility to ensure that such observations were made, that failure of the defendant to observe the patient for a 40-minute period was a "deviation from good and acceptable nursing practice and psychiatric and mental health nursing practice," and that the defendant's conduct was a "contributing cause of death."

After reviewing the fact pattern and judicial reasoning, one might question whether any of the nurses involved in Mrs. Delicata's care understood that one measure of legal accountability is the skill with which they use their knowledge of psychiatric nursing to develop a therapeutic nurse-patient relationship. That nursing conduct cannot be isolated from the law will be illustrated as we bring together nursing conduct and judicial reasoning in an assessment of the care given to Mrs. Carmela Delicata.

Analyzing the nursing conduct to which the legal principles applied

A first step in analyzing the nursing conduct in this situation is to question what action should have been taken when a continuing acceptance of medical orders and opinion ran counter to patient safety and a legally acceptable standard of care. Is it the duty of the nurse to question the colleague physician regarding the reasons for the order? Professional nurses are independent practitioners, legally accountable for implementing an acceptable standard of care, irrespective of opinions from related professional groups; failing in this task places them in legal jeopardy.

In reviewing the circumstances that culminated in Mrs. Delicata's death, the failure of the nursing staff to take appropriate steps to avoid harm appears not to be due to their failure to assess the worsening state of the patient's mental health, but to their failure to use their observations effectively in providing an acceptable standard of psychiatric nursing care. With any suicidal patient, the most satisfactory intervention is prevention, i.e., providing a safe environment in which the patient feels valued and secure.

The nurses' notes show that the staff was aware of the patient's feelings of helplessness and worthlessness. Her first attempt at suicide in the presence of her daughter and her plea for assistance from the staff in taking her own life should have been seen as a cry for help, a conflict in her desire to live and her wish to end a life with which she could not cope. The staff reacted by placing Mrs. Delicata under constant supervision— action that could be considered an initial step in acceptable nursing conduct. However, one must consider what else should have been done. Was the supervision sufficiently supportive to alleviate the emotional pain the patient was undergoing, or was it the kind of surveillance that would cause the patient to feel that she was being punished for trying to destroy herself? And, even though this action had been, at an earlier time, judged to be unnecessary by a staff psychologist and a staff psychiatrist, why did the nursing staff continue to rely on these orders? Why did they not allow their professional judgment to guide them in providing an environment in which the patient could be protected from self-destructive impulses yet free to explore in a therapeutic relationship her feelings of worthlessness? Had they adhered to their original plan, the death for which nurse Bourlesses may ultimately be held accountable might have been prevented.

When Mrs. Delicata resisted the suggestion that she would benefit from electroshock therapy, "reassurance was not helpful." Without further detail it is impossible to assess accurately the reassurance that was given. However, since Mrs. Delicata did exhibit a rapidly worsening condition, one might conclude that little had been done up to this point to help her deal with her feelings or to establish a trusting relationship. Reassurance comes only after a person feels that others are truly interested and that it is safe to talk out one's concerns without fear of further loss of self-esteem. Similarly, there is nothing in the record to indicate that the staff took any action when a fellow patient reported the apparent rejection of Mrs. Delicata by her husband on the evening of her death. One can only speculate that nursing intervention that would have helped her cope with the loss of support she must have been experiencing might have eliminated, in part, the stress that drove her to her final suicidal act. At the very least, it was a clue that the patient needed much closer supervision and support than had been judged to be necessary by the medical staff 3 days prior to her death.

The court made plain the fact that possible negligence on the part of other personnel charged with care of the deceased in no way relieved the liability for the harm done by the responsible nurse. It is a significant legal decision to hold the nurse accountable for failure to use the knowledge and skills of a professional psychiatric nurse in developing and sustaining a plan of care based on continuing reassessment of patient needs.

MIRHOSSEINY V. BOARD OF SUPERVISORS OF LOUISIANA STATE UNIVERSITY AND AGRICULTURAL AND MECHANICAL COLLEGE[2]

Action was brought against board of supervisors of state university, nurse employed in university's infirmary, insurer and manufacturer of antibiotic drug for injuries resulting from intramuscular injection plaintiff student received at infirmary. The court entered a judgment rejecting the claim and the plaintiff filed an appeal.

This is an appeal by Allmire Mirhosseiny, plaintiff appellant, of a judgment rejecting his claim for tort damages against the Board of Supervisors of Louisiana State University and Agricultural and Mechanical College, Mrs. Grace K. Cooney, St. Paul Fire and Marine Insurance Company, and American Home Products Corporation, defendants-appellees, resulting from an intramuscular injection he received in the right buttock at the Louisiana Student Infirmary on November 1, 1973. Plaintiff, a 23 year old foreign student, was enrolled at Louisiana State University. The injection was the third in a series of monthly injections of Bicillin L-A (a long-lasting antibiotic drug) prescribed by his Iranian physician and administered by Mrs. Grace K. Cooney, a nurse at the facility. Soon after the injection the plaintiff returned to the infirmary with intense pain in his right leg. He was treated immediately, but required hospitalization at the infirmary for several weeks. There, he was treated by Doctors Addis and Luikart and later was seen by Doctors Levert and Kline both of whom were neurologists.

At trial there was no dispute between the parties that plaintiff's disability resulted from the hypodermic injection, nor was there any dispute that the bicillin was an irritant to the sciatic nerve.

Appellant's first argument is that the doctrine of *Res Ipsa Loquitur* should have been applied by the trial court under the circumstances of this case. It is well established in the Louisiana jurisprudence that the maxim, res ipsa loquitur, is properly applied when the accident is of a kind that does not ordinarily occur in the absence of negligence; the injury was caused by an agency or instrumentality within the control of the defendant; and evidence as to the cause of the accident is more readily available to the defendant.

> [T]he maxim means only that the facts of the occurrence warrant the inference of negligence, not that they compel such an inference; that the rule rests for its justification upon the common experience that accidents from such causes do not commonly occur in the absence of negligence; and that it is the lack of direct evidence indicating negligence on the part of the defendant as the responsible human cause of a particular accident which actually furnishes the necessity for invoking the rule in its strict and distinctive sense.
>
> All that is meant by res ipsa loquitur is that the circumstances involved in or connected with an accident are of such an unusual character as to justify, in the absence of other evidence bearing on the subject, the inference that the accident was due to the negligence of the one having control of the thing which caused the injury. This inference is not drawn merely because the thing speaks for itself, but because all of the circumstances surrounding the accident are of such a character that, unless an explanation can be given, the only fair and reasonable conclusion is that the accident was due to some omission of the defendant's duty.

From the medical expert testimony in the record it appears that the type of injury suffered by the plaintiff in this case could have been caused by injecting bicillin directly into the sciatic nerve or by injecting bicillin around or on the sciatic nerve, both of which would involve a deviation from the standard of care in such cases. A third possibility assumes an injection conforming with the standard of care and having the bicillin "filter" to the sciatic nerve thus causing the injury.

The standard of care in the Baton Rouge community applicable to "shot nurses" for buttock injections is that the injection be given in the upper outside quadrant and at a ninety degree angle to the surface of the skin.

There was also direct evidence introduced as to the location of the point of injection and as to the angle of penetration.

From the foregoing, it is apparent that the Trial Judge had sufficient direct evidence presented to preclude the application of res ipsa loquitur. Further there was testimony by medical experts that, though infrequent, this type of injury can occur even in the absence of any negligence.

Plaintiff's last specification of error is that the Trial Court erred in rendering judgment in favor of all defendants. In its reasons for judgment the Trial Judge found:

> The plaintiff was a very frail, thin, emaciated individual. It was shown that a person of his build and physique is more prone to suffer this type of injury than a well nourished supple individual. It was more or less agreed between the medical experts that there was no direct hit of the sciatic nerve, but that undoubtedly the medicine (bicillin) infiltrated through the muscle planes and enveloped or least reached the nerve and caused the resulting injury and disability. Had the nerve been hit, a direct blow by the needle, the fact would have been instantly reported by the plaintiff. . . . In view of the plaintiff's physique, the testimony of Doctors Addis, Kline and Luikart as to what more likely occurred that, the positive finding of Dr. Addis and the testimony of Mrs. Cooney, this court finds that the plaintiff has not sustained his burden of proof that Mrs. Cooney was negligent in the administration of the bicillin, or that she violated the two-fold standard of care.

In a deposition taken by Dr. David G. Kline, a neurosurgeon, he stated that, particularly with the sciatic nerve, some patients who fit the description of the plaintiff's physique may experience a delayed onset of this difficulty due to the medication being deposited in an anatomical plane leading to the nerve allowing it to bathe the nerve over a period of time extending from minutes to hours. That evidence was supported by Dr. C. Bryan Luikart, Jr. who stated in his deposition that filtration to the nerve is possible even at a distance from the point of injection. Even plaintiff's expert neurologist, Dr. Sam L. Levert, Jr., testified that the filtration idea was logical and that it is a theory only in that no one has ever actually seen it occur, and that its reasonableness is supported by the many instances in which persons feel no pain until the passage of one, five or ten minutes or as much as an hour or longer after the administration of the injection.

There was testimony by Dr. Barrelle N. Addis that the site of the injection was located in the upper outside quadrant of the buttock. Mrs. Cooney also testified that she administered the injection in the upper outside quadrant at a ninety degree angle which testimony was accepted by the Trial Judge.

We find that the record amply supports the conclusions and the judgment of the Trial Court.

The evidence in the record establishes that there was nothing wrong with the bicillin and the judgment in favor of American Home Products Corporation, manufacturer of the bicillin, is correct.

For these reasons, the judgment of the Trial Court is affirmed.

Examining the fact pattern

The fact pattern in this instance is uncomplicated. The plaintiff, All-mire Mirhosseiny, a student at Louisiana State University, was undergoing a treatment regimen at the University Infirmary which necessitated the administration of intramuscular injections of long-acting bicillin. The third injection was administered by Mrs. Grace K. Cooney, a nurse at the facility, at a ninety-degree angle into the upper outer quadrant of the right buttock. Soon after the injection, Mirhosseiny returned to the infirmary complaining of intense pain in his right leg. He was treated immediately and hospitalized for several weeks, during which time he was seen by two neurologists.

Identifying the legal principles used in the judicial decision

Action was brought in district court by the student, Allmire Mirhosseiny, against the Board of Supervisors of the University, Nurse Cooney, and the insurer and manufacturer of the drug for injuries resulting from the intramuscular injection. The district court entered judgment rejecting the claim, and an appeal was filed by the plaintiff arguing that the doctrine of *res ipsa loquitur* should have been applied by the trial court.

The appeals court held that there was sufficient direct evidence to preclude application of *res ipsa loquitur* in view of the expert medical testimony "that, though infrequent, such type of injury can occur even in the absence of any negligence." Although there was no dispute that the plaintiff's disability resulted from irritation to the sciatic nerve caused by the bicillin injection, the court held that the method of injection used by Mrs. Cooney in administering the drug met an acceptable standard of care. Her testimony relative to the technique used was supported by that of Dr. Addis, one of Mirhosseiny's physicians.

In reaching their finding that the evidence supported the judgment of the trial court, the appeals court relied also on the expert medical testimony of Doctors Levert and Kline, neurologists. In the opinion of these experts, medication injected into the muscles of the buttock can infiltrate through muscle planes, reach the sciatic nerve, and cause irritation and possible injury. This phenomenon is more likely to occur in thin, emaciated persons, like the plaintiff, than in well-nourished individuals. Furthermore, they contended, had the drug been injected directly into the nerve, the patient would have complained of pain instantly.

Analyzing nursing conduct to which the legal principles applied

In examining the circumstances that brought Nurse Cooney's conduct to the attention of the court, nurses should reflect on the knowledge base underlying common nursing procedures and techniques. Often, they perform techniques such as intramuscular injections many times in the course of a single tour of duty, a practice that could lead to rote performance rather than a thorough appraisal of the patient, the drug, and the technique of administration.

The administration of intramuscular injections necessitates adequate exposure of the injection site and careful mapping and palpating to locate the bone structure that guides the nurse in identifying injection sites normally free of large nerve or blood vessels. Should injury occur, nurses charged with negligence have as their best defense the knowledge that they can testify to the fact that the technique used in administering the drug complied with an acceptable standard of care, which could be further supported by testimony of a nurse expert witness.

As explained by the expert medical witnesses in the case previously cited, it is possible, particularly in a thin, emaciated person, for a drug to infiltrate muscle planes to envelop the sciatic nerve, resulting in pain and possible disability. The nurse who is aware of this theory can help protect the patient by careful assessment of the injection site and by discussing with the physician the problems inherent in long-term therapy by the intramuscular route. Furthermore, nurses may protect themselves from a charge of negligence by accurately recording both the time the injection was given and the time the patient first complained of pain since, if the drug were injected directly into the nerve, the pain would be instantaneous.

Analysis of litigated cases involving nurses serves many purposes. It causes the profession to examine its practice from the unbiased position of the courts. It provides tested legal principles on which to base future nursing judgments. It forces nurses and employers of nursing to reflect on the maintenance of an acceptable standard of care in order to avoid future litigation. It should prompt nurse educators to identify a core of legal content for integration into nursing curricula. And, last but not least, it brings into sharper focus the right of the patient to receive the best care that modern science and a humanistically oriented society can provide.

THE CASE THAT NEVER WENT TO COURT

Since health care delivery is a complex process, questions of negligence or violation of patient's rights will inevitably be raised from time to time. It is likely that most of these incidents will soon be forgotten. Few probably should or will go on to determination by the courts. However, in the interest of improving care and of defining more explicitly the autonomous functions of nursing, instances of questionable nursing conduct should not be overlooked. Nurses, whether or not they are involved, should acknowledge that a patient care problem exists and make every effort to determine why it occurred and how similar incidents could be avoided in the future.

Once the problem has been defined, the three-step method offered for analysis of a litigated case can be modified for use in assessing nursing accountability. The technique then becomes primarily a tool for peer review by examining nursing conduct in terms of legal principles. The outcome of such a procedure should be better service for health care recipients and a better understanding of the position of the nurse in the health care system.

The following incident illustrates how subjecting a patient care situation to a legally oriented analysis can lead to the fixing of nursing accountability and to suggestions for preventing a similar episode in the future.

Mr. Job's arrest

Mr. Job was admitted to the coronary care unit on Monday evening. On admission he complained of pain in the left chest radiating down the left arm. His diagnosis was possible myocardial infarction. Intravenous lidocaine therapy was initiated and continued throughout the night. By Tuesday morning he was free of pain. His monitor pattern showed a normal sinus rhythm with three to four unifocal premature ventricular contractions per minute. At 10:00 A.M. he was visited by his physician, who discontinued the intravenous therapy and left an order for transfer to a medical unit.

The nurses' notes for Tuesday read as follows:

7:00 A.M. to 10:00 A.M.	Morning care. Appetite good. Denies pain. In NSR with occasional PVCs (monitor strip attached). In chair—tolerated well.
10:30 A.M.	Transferred to Room 806 by wheelchair.
1:00 P.M. to 3:00 P.M.	Enjoyed lunch. Resting well. Visited with family.

At 3:30 P.M. Mr. Job's roommate called for help. The nurse who responded to the call immediately recognized that Mr. Job was in cardiac arrest.

Resuscitation measures were successful, and Mr. Job was later moved back to the coronary care unit.

Mr. Job's roommate, who was also a cardiac patient, was greatly disturbed by the incident. He reported that at about 3:00 P.M. Job had told a nurse's aide that he was having chest pain. She said she would tell the charge nurse as soon as the nurses finished with shift report.

Analyzing the fact pattern

Extracting the significant facts in the case of Mr. Job is relatively simple. A patient with a diagnosis of possible myocardial infarction was transferred from the coronary care unit to a medical unit at 10:30 A.M. He was pain-free at the time of the transfer and was known to be in normal sinus rhythm but with occasional premature ventricular contractions. At 3:00 P.M. he complained of chest pain, but the complaint was not communicated to the professional nursing staff. There was no record of cardiac assessment from 10:00 A.M. until the patient arrested.

Applying relevant legal principles

STANDARD OF CARE. The patient record indicated that Mr. Job, a patient under observation for possible myocardial infarction, received no direct professional nursing care from the time of his transfer to Room 806 until he arrested at 3:30 P.M. From this it could be concluded that the staff failed to exercise due care in observing and evaluating the patient.

The fact that the nurse's aide did not immediately communicate the patient's complaint of pain suggested a failure on the part of the professional staff to give proper guidance to their ancillary personnel.

DUTY TO FORESEE HARM. Since Mr. Job had been diagnosed as a possible myocardial infarction and since he was showing occasional premature ventricular contractions, his record should have shown some evidence of cardiac assessment. Neglecting to evaluate the status of such a patient implied failure to foresee, and possibly forestall, harm.

Identifying accountability

The conduct of the professional nursing staff on the medical unit was wanting because they failed to provide adequate supervision for a patient undergoing evaluation for myocardial infarction. Although nursing assessment may not have detected evidence of impending arrest, the actions of the professional nursing staff failed to meet generally accepted criteria for the care of an acutely ill cardiac patient.

As an outgrowth of the inquiry, the procedure for transfer of patients between hospital units was reviewed. The need for more effective communication between staff and between doctors and nurses was explored, and plans were made to ensure a more patient-oriented approach to the transfer procedure. Furthermore, it was decided that the professional staff of the medical unit would profit from an in-service program geared to the particular needs of the acutely ill cardiac patient. As often happens when a patient record is studied, the nursing notes were judged to be irrelevant and lacking in factual data. This led to steps being taken to investigate this important adjunct to care throughout the entire institution.

As nursing gains in professional stature and becomes more skilled in analyzing and judging its own conduct, reporting will become more precise and the functions of the profession will become more clearly defined. Practitioners will enjoy the security of knowing the parameters within which they are free to operate, and the patients they serve will benefit from care that is personal, competent, and legally sound.

12

Accountability—the full-time partner of autonomy

In nursing and at the interface of law and nursing, considerable emphasis is placed on individual responsibility, making informed and mature judgments, and carrying out nursing tasks based on an in-depth understanding of physical, biologic, and psychologic processes. Indeed, individual responsibility is the touchstone of modern nursing and a major contributing factor to the expansion of nursing's role to degrees of sophistication undreamed of a short time ago.

Emergence of this individual responsibility was not accidental. It was the foresight of nursing leaders who, against great odds, moved nursing out of its apprenticeship training to academic settings that made possible the interdisciplinary base on which professional practice could be built. This knowledge base, grounded in the physical, biologic, and social sciences, is generally accepted in statutory definitions of nursing as a requirement for developing the judgment and skills necessary to carry out its functions. And it is this judgment and skill that make possible the nursing conduct that will come under scrutiny in the event a problem arises and the legal process is evoked.

How does this picture of the professional nurse square with the idea that the nurse may be an employee bound to an employer in a paternalistic relationship, whereby the employer becomes responsible for the nurse's acts? The answer is simple but nonetheless frequently subject to misinterpretation. Independent judgment and professional sophistication have little to do with whether or not a nurse is an employee or whether liability for nursing conduct can be vicariously extended to an employer. In a legal sense an employer-employee relationship exists where the employee operates in a place furnished by the employer, carries out tasks in a broad sense determined by the employer, and receives compensation from the employer. It is for these reasons alone that legal liability will be imposed on the employer in the event of an employee error. It is the relationship and not the character of the act, that is, whether it required a high degree of judgment and skill or whether it was in response to another's direction, that determines vicarious liability.

THE MYTH OF DEPENDENT FUNCTIONING IN PROFESSIONAL NURSING

The functions of nursing have often been categorized as dependent or independent. Perhaps the time has arrived when professional nursing should move away from such semantic exercises. As we have said earlier, nurses are professionals and, as such, have no dependent functions. Whether they conduct an independent practice with their own clientele, whether they function in an interdpendent relationship with professional colleagues, or whether they operate in a hierarchical structure where the organizational chart shows them in a subordinate position to others, they are all independent practitioners.

All are autonomous in that they are qualified to make decisions and act responsibly in their own interests and in the interests of others. Even though they carry out a medical regimen prescribed by a physician-colleague, they do so with the understanding that they are responsible for assessing the appropriateness of any or all parts of the regimen if the circumstances under which it was prescribed are altered. The mandate that states the nurse must not alter the medical regimen might well be modified to read "unless the condition of the patient dictates that you do so." But autonomy does not come cheaply; the price to be paid is accountability.

SHARING THE ACCOUNTABILITY FOR NURSING ACTS

Accountability is a strange commodity. It can be shared, yet it does not diminish. Previously we explored how and why the employing institution shares the legal accountability with its nursing employees. Now we are about to consider a more positive side of shared accountability. When two persons share the responsibility or accountability for a decision or action, neither one is less legally accountable for its outcome. Yet sharing reduces the burden; by adding another person's judgment into the decision-making process, margin for error is reduced.

Nurses who fly solo in independent practice have less opportunity for sharing ideas and decisions with colleagues. They do, however, have access to the most important person with whom any nurse can share accountability—the patient. Through disclosure the nurse allows the patient to join in decisions about his care and treatment, which are rightly his to make, and in so doing he also becomes accountable. Nursing accountability does not lessen, however, for the very act of disclosure carries with it accountability. Yet it is likely that disclosure will minimize the legal risk for the nurse, for undoubtedly the patient's involvement causes him to become more accepting of the care he receives.

The nurse who functions in an interdependent relationship with other health care professionals is in a most fortunate position. In the process of sharing, a collective wisdom emerges, which in all probability lessens the risk to the patient. This sharing of professional judgment and skill cannot in any sense reduce individual accountability, but it usually lowers the potential for legal liability should the outcome of an action be less than favorable.

Nurses who, through supervisory functions, delegate responsibility and with it accountability to students and ancillary personnel admittedly share at greater risk than those who share with persons equally qualified. The goal of supervision, however, is to bring each person supervised to his optimum level of functioning, as near as possible to the level of independent action. Operating from this frame of reference, supervisory nurses extend themselves through the actions of others. Yet they must always recognize that their accountability is great, for it extends not only to the patient but to the success or failure of the person supervised. This does not imply the supervisor is liable for another's negligence or that the supervisee could hold the supervisor liable for failure to succeed in nursing. Under our system of justice, everyone is responsible for his own acts.

Finally, nursing accountability projects into the future. Each professional shares in the accountability for what nursing becomes and for the services it will offer to yet unidentified clientele. If the character of the profession is to continue to be shaped by those who know its strengths and weaknesses best, nurses must be alert to all the social forces that exert influence on the practice of nursing.

Not the least of these is law. For it is through statutory law that nursing practice is legally defined and its practitioners are licensed and controlled. It is through tort law that nursing actions that have come under scrutiny are judged by those outside the profession. Litigation involving nursing conduct has a message for nursing that all professional nurses should heed.

ACCOUNTABILITY AS A MEASURE OF LIABILITY

Life without action, either intellectual or physical, would indeed be no life at all. Similarly, an inactive profession ceases to be a profession. Nursing will only grow in depth and in the extension of its services through its actions. Nurses must accept, however, that they are always accountable for their actions; in the event a patient is harmed, nursing accountability becomes a measure of legal liability. Accountability implies duty and that a reasonable standard of care will be taken in the exercise of that duty. The nurse who has learned to meld nursing and relevant legal concepts in the nursing process will not be threatened by accountability as a measure of legal liability. For these nurses, legal accountability will be one measure of a job well done and the key to improving nursing practice.

References

Introduction and Section one

1. Anderson, E.H., Bergerson, B.S., Duffey, M., Lohr, M., and Rose, M.H., editors: Current concepts in clinical nursing, vol. 4, St. Louis, 1973, The C.V. Mosby Co., p. 321.

2. Merton, R.K.: The functions of the professional association, Am. J. Nurs. **58**:50, 1958.

3. Platform of American Nurses Association, Am. J. Nurs. **52**:953, 1952.

4. American Nurses' Association: Suggestions for major provisions to be included in a nursing practice act which is mandatory for professional nursing, Section II, b, 1958.

5. Hall, V.C.: Statutory regulation of the scope of nursing practice, National Joint Practice Commission, Chicago, 1975, John Hancock Center, p. 22.

6. *Leib v. Board of Examiners for Nursing of State of Connecticut,* 177 Conn. 78, 411 A.2d 42 (1979).

7. *Tuma v. Board of Nursing of State of Idaho,* 100 Idaho 74, 593 P.2d 711 (1979).

8. Murchison, I.A., and Nichols, T.S.: Legal foundations of nursing practice, New York, 1970, The Macmillan Co., p. 13.

9. Wormser, R.: The law: the story of lawmakers and the law we live by, New York, 1949, Simon & Schuster, Inc., pp. 16-20.

10. Murchison and Nichols, op. cit., p. 72.

11. Pound, R.: Interpretations of legal history, Cambridge, England, 1922.

12. *Stemmer v. Kline,* 128 N.J.L. 455, 26 A.2d 489 (1942). The rule adopted in 1942 in *Stemmer v. Kline* was changed 18 years later in *Smith v. Brennan,* 31 N.J. 353, 157 A.2d 497 (1960).

13. *Williams v. Marion Rapid Transit, Inc.,* 152 Ohio St. 114, 87 N.E.2d 334 (1949).

14. *Cooper v. National Motor Bearing Co.,* 136 Cal. App. 2d 299, 288 P.2d 581 (1955).

15. *Gugino v. Harvard Community Health Plan,* 403 N.E.2d 1166 (1980).

16. *Applebaum v. Board of Directors of Barton Memorial Hospital,* 104 Cal. App. 3d 648, 163 Cal. Rptr. 831 (1980).
17. *Darling v. Charleston Community Memorial Hospital,* 33 Ill. 2d 326, 211 N.E.2d 253 (1966).
18. *Cooper v. National Motor Bearing Co.,* 136 Cal. App. 2d 299, 288 P.2d 581 (1955).

Section two

1. Gregory, C.O., and Kalven, H., Jr.: Cases and materials on torts, Boston, 1959, Little, Brown & Co., p. 89.
2. Standards of Nursing Practice, American Nurses' Association, 1973.
3. *Jones v. Hawkes Hospital,* 175 Ohio St. 503, 196 N.E.2d 592 (1964).
4. *Goff v. Doctors General Hospital,* 166 Cal. App. 2d 314, 333 P.2d 29 (1958).
5. Dachelet, C.Z., and Sullivan, J.A.: Autonomy in practice, Nurs. Pract. **4**(2): 19, 1979.
6. *Brown v. Shannon West Texas Memorial Hospital,* 222 S.W.2d 248 (Tex. Civ. App. 1949).
7. Federal·Food, Drug and Cosmetic Act, 21 U.S.C. §§ 301-92.
8. Testimony of George P. Larrick, Commissioner of Food and Drugs, 1961-66, at Hearings on Drug Safety Before the Subcomm. on Intergovernmental Relations of the House Comm. on Government Operations, 88th Congress, 2d Session, pt. 1, at 147 (1964).
9. *Reyes v. Wyeth Laboratories,* 498 F.2d 1264 (5th Cir. 1974).
10. *Mahr v. G.D. Searle & Co.,* 72 Ill. App. 3d 540, 390 N.E.2d 1214 (1979).
11. *Richard v. S.W. Louisiana Hospital Association,* 383 So. 2d 83 (1980).
12. *Ybarra v. Spangard,* 25 Cal. 2d 486, 154 P.2d 687 (1944).
13. *Hiatt v. Groce,* 215 Kan. 14, 523 P.2d 320 (1974).
14. Eccard, W.T.: A revolution in white—new approaches in treating nurses as professionals, Vanderbilt Law Rev. **30:**865-866, 1977.
15. *Darling v. Charleston Community Memorial Hospital,* 33 Ill. 2d 253 (1966).

Section three

1. American Nurses' Association: Code for nurses with interpretive statements, 1976.
2. American Hospital Association: A patient's bill of rights, 1973.
3. Murchison, I.A., and Nichols, T.S.: Legal foundations of nursing practices, New York, 1970, The Macmillan Co., p. 283.
4. Carter, F.M.: Psychosocial nursing, ed. 2, New York, 1976, The Macmillan Co., p. 510.
5. Colorado Statutes, Sec. 25-1-120, 1976.
6. Woodham-Smith, C.: Florence Nightingale, New York, 1951, McGraw-Hill Book Co., p. 226.
7. *Schloendorff v. Society of New York Hospital,* 211 N.Y. 125, 105 N.E. 92 (1914).
8. *Goedecke v. State of Colorado, Department of Institutions,* 603 P.2d 123 (1979).

Section four

1. *Delicata v. Bourlesses*, 404 N.E.2d 667 (1980).
2. *Mirhosseiny v. Board of Supervisors of Louisiana State University*, 351 So. 2d 1318 (1977).

Index

A

Accountability, 1-3
  autonomy and, 176-179
  common law of torts and, 56-60
  dependent functioning and, 177
  liability and, 179
  sharing of, for nursing acts, 177-179
Affirmative action, 75-76
American Hospital Association *Patient's Bill of Rights,* 129-131
American Nurses' Association
  Code for Nurses of, 128
  model Nurse Practice Act and, 17-18
  standards for professional nursing practice and, 65
  voluntary controls and, 14-15
Applebaum v. Board of Directors of Barton Memorial Hospital, 56
Authority, 1-3
Autonomy, 176-179

B

Board of nursing
  judicial review and, 35-38
  safeguards and, 39-44
  sanctions and, 33

C

Care standards, 63-73
  American Nurses' Association and, 65
  in nursing process, 65-67, 69-73
  for reasonably prudent nurse, 64
  risk taking and, 66-67, 68-69
Causation of injury, 84-103
  drug liability and, 90-92
  multiple, 86-87
  nursing action and, 97-102
  products liability and, 87-88
    causal relationships and, 93-94
    failure to warn and, 89-90
    nursing role in, 92-93
  proof of, 85-86
  res ipsa loquitur and, 94-96
Code for Nurses, 128

Colleague relationships, 77-78
Common law, 45-60
  accountability and, 56-60
  malpractice and, 49-51
  negligence and, 49-51
  precedent in, 51-52
    departure from, 54-55
    nursing conduct and, 52-54
  scope and meaning of, 46-47
  tort law and, 46-48
    accountability and, 56-60
    liability and, 48-49
Conduct, nursing; *see* Nursing conduct
Consent, 144-156
  disclosure and, 146-149
  importance of, 152-155
  informed, 149-150
    forms and, 150-151
  patient involvement and, 147-148
  relinquishment of rights and, 144-146
  source of, 150
  verbal, 151-152
Consent forms, 150-151
Constitution of United States, 127-128
Consumer control of nursing conduct, 13-32
  history of, 17-18
  legal boundaries for, 19
  nursing law and, 25-32
  nursing practitioner and, 25-32
  practice acts and
    medical, 22-24
    nurse, 19, 20-22
  voluntary controls and, 14-16
Corporate liability, 115-118

D

Delicata v. Bourlesses, 159-168
Direct liability, 115-118
Disciplinary action, 33-44
  board of nursing and
    decision of, 35-38
    safeguards and, 39-44
  hypothetical analysis and, 38-39
  legal and judicial review and, 34-38

Disclosure
  as basis for consent, 146-147
  limitations on, 148-149
  patient involvement and, 147-148
Drugs
  federal law and, 88
  liability and, 90-92
Duty of nurse, legal, 9, 74-83
  affirmative action and, 75-76
  colleagues and, 77-78
  to eliminate risks, 76-77
  to foresee harm, 76-77, 78-82

E

Employer-employee liability, 114-123
  corporate liability and, 115-118
  direct liability and, 115-118
  distance as risk factor in, 119-122
  student conduct and, 118-119
  vicarious liability and, 114-115
Expansion of nursing process, proposal for,
  3-6
Expert witness, 106-107
  future nursing practice and, 109-113
  nurse as, 107-109

F

Food, Drug and Cosmetic Act, 88
Foreseeability, 8-9, 76-77, 78-82
Freedon from intrusion, 127-143
  intentional intrusion and, 131-132
  mental illness or incompetence and,
    134-135
  nursing duty versus, 135-142
  patient rights and, 127-131
  responsiblity for, 133-134

G

Goedecke v. Department of Institutions,
  145-146
Goff v. Doctors General Hospital, 76
*Gugino v. Harvard Community Health
  Plan,* 55-56

H

Harm, foreseeing potential for, 8-9, 76-77,
  78-79
Hiatt v. Groce, 108
History of legal controls, 17-18

I

Illinois Supreme Court, 117
Incompetence, rights and, 134-135
Informed consent, 149-150
  forms for, 150-151
Injury, causation of; *see* Causation of injury
Institutional liability, 114-115
Intrusion, freedom from, 127-143
  intentional intrusion and, 131-132
  mental illness or incompetence and, 134-
    135
  nursing duty versus, 135-142
  patient rights and, 127-131
  responsibility for, 133-134

J

Judicial review of board decision, 35-38

L

Law
  common; *see* Common law
  nursing process and, 6-10
Legal analysis of nursing conduct, 158-175
  Delicata v. Bourlesses and, 159-168
  *Mirhosseiny v. Board of Supervisors of
    Louisiana State University and Ag-
    ricultural and Mechanical College*
    and, 168-173
Legal controls, 17-18
Legal duty of nurse, 9, 74-83; *see also*
    Nursing; Nursing conduct
  affirmative action and, 75-76
  colleagues and, 77-78
  to eliminate risks, 76-77
  for foresee harm, 76-77, 78-82

Legal grounds for disciplinary action, 33-44
  board of nursing and
    decision of, 35-38
    safeguards and, 39-44
  hypothetical analysis and, 38-39
  legal and judicial review and, 34-38
*Leib v. Board of Examiners for Nursing of
  State of Connecticut,* 35-36
Liability
  common law and, 48-49
  corporate, 115-118
  direct, 115-118
  drug, 90-92
  employer-employee; *see* Employer-em-
    ployee liability
  of institution, 114-115
  products; *see* Products liability
  for torts, 48-49
Licensure, 17
  revocation of, 43-44

M

Mahr v. G.D. Searle & Co., 91-92
Malpractice, 49-51
Mandatory licensure, 17
  revocation and, 43-44
Medical practice act, 22-24
Mental illness or incompetence, rights and,
  134-135
*Mirhosseiny v. Board of Supervisors of
  Louisiana State University and Ag-
  ricultural and Mechanical College,*
  168-173
Multiple causation, 86-87

N

Negligence, 49-51, 74-75
  employer-employee liability for
    corporate liability and, 115-118
    direct liability and, 115-118
    distance as risk factor in, 119-122
    student conduct and, 118-119
    vicarious liability and, 114-115

Nightingale, F., 142-143
Notes on Hospitals, 142-143
Nurse; *see also* Nursing; Nursing conduct
  legal duty of; *see* Duty of nurse, legal
  physician and, overlapping function of,
    24-25
  reasonably prudent, 64
  as risk taker, 68-69
  as witness, 104-113
Nurse practice acts, 17-18, 19-22
Nursing; *see also* Nurse; Nursing conduct
  board of
    judicial review and, 35-38
    safeguards and, 39-44
    sanctions and, 33
  harmful action and, 97-102
  patient rights and, 135-142
  and proposal for expansion, 3-6
Nursing conduct; *see also* Nurse; Nursing
  control of, 13-32
    history and, 17-18
    legal boundaries for, 19-22
    medical practice act and, 22-24
    nurse practice act and, 19, 20-22
    nursing law and, 25-32
    nursing practitioner and, 25-32
    voluntary, 14-16
  legal analysis of, 158-175
    Delicata v. Bourlesses and, 159-168
    *Mirhosseiny v. Board of Supervisors of
    Louisiana State University and Ag-
    ricultural and Mechanical College*
    and, 168-173

P

Pathfinder case, 54
Patient rights; *see* Rights of patient
Patient's Bill of Rights, 129-131
Peer review, 33-34
Physical intrusion, 131-132
Physician, nursing functions and, 24-25
Precedent, 51-52
  departure from, 54-55

Precedent—cont'd
nursing conduct and, 52-54
Privacy, right of, 133
Products liability, 87-88
causal relationships and, 93-94
failure to warn and, 89-90
nursing role in, 92-93
Professional associations, 14-16
Proof of causation, 85-86

R

Reasonably prudent nurse, 64
Relinquishment of rights, 144-146
Reprimand, board of nursing and, 39-41
Res ipsa loquitur, 94-96
Revocation of license, 43-44
Reyes v. Wyeth Laboratories, 90-91
*Richard v. Southwest Louisiana Hospital
Association,* 92-93
Rights of patient, 9, 125-156
American Hospital Association and, 129-
131
to consent, 144-156; *see also* Consent
to freedom from intrusion, 127-143; *see
also* Freedom from intrusion
meaning and scope of, 127-131
mental illness or incompetence and,
134-135
nursing duty versus, 135-142
to privacy, 133
relinquishment of, 144-146
responsibility for, 133-134
Risks
elimination of, 76-77
taking of, 66-67, 68-69

S

Sanctions, 33
Standards of care, 63-73
of American Nurses' Association, 65
in nursing process, 65-67, 69-73
for reasonably prudent nurse, 64
risk taking and, 66-67, 68-69
Standards for Hospital Accreditation of
Joint Commission on Accreditation,
117
Stare decisis, 51
Student conduct, 118-119
Substantial factor test, 85-86
Suspension, board of nursing and, 41-43

T

Torts, 46-48
accountability and, 56-60
liability and, 48-49
Tuma v. Board of Nursing, State of Ohio,
36-38

V

Verbal consent, 151-152
Vicarious liability, 114-115
Voluntary controls, 14-16

W

Witnesses, 104-113
expert, 106-109
future nursing practice and, 109-113

Y

Ybarra v. Spangard, 96